8782161

WARREN

Vanishing Street
Furniture

711.6

£7·50

HERTFORDSHIRE LIBRARY SERVICE

Please return this book on or before the date shown below or ask for
it to be renewal. Applications for renewal by post
or tele formation on
the number on
the d or which
are y bringing
ther in demand.

L.32A

Please renew/return this item by the last date shown.

So that your telephone call is charged at local rate,
please call the numbers as set out below:

	From Area codes 01923 or 0208:	From the rest of Herts:
Renewals:	01923 471373	01438 737373
Enquiries:	01923 471333	01438 737333
Minicom:	01923 471599	01438 737599

L32b

JUL 1980
DEC 1980

MAR 1981

OCT 1978   JUN 1979   APR 1981

KU-487-907

Vanishing Street Furniture

By the same author:

A Stitch in Time - Victorian and Edwardian Needlecraft
The All Colour Book of Art Nouveau
Royal Souvenirs

Vanishing Street Furniture

Geoffrey Warren

David & Charles
Newton Abbot   London   North Pomfret (Vt)   Vancouver

For Barbara

Warren, Geoffrey
  Vanishing street furniture.
  1. Streets - Great Britain - Accessories
  I. Title
  620.4'17'32   TE 57

  ISBN 0-7153-7482-6

Library of Congress Catalog Card Number : 77-85020.

© Geoffrey Warren 1978
All rights reserved. No part of this
publication may be reproduced, stored
in a retrieval system, or transmitted, in
any form or by any means, electronic,
mechanical, photocopying, recording or
otherwise, without the prior permission
of David & Charles (Publishers) Limited

Set by HBM Typesetting Limited
Standish Street Chorley Lancashire
and Printed in Great Britain
by Biddles Limited Guildford Surrey
for David & Charles (Publishers) Limited
Brunel House Newton Abbot Devon

Published in the United States of America
by David & Charles Inc
North Pomfret Vermont 05053 USA

Published in Canada
by Douglas David & Charles Limited
1875 Welch Street North Vancouver BC

HERTFORDSHIRE
LIBRARY SERVICE
711.6
8782161

Contents

Introduction 9

1 Well watered 16

2 A sound of coolness in the busy street 39

3 Convenient 66

4 All lit up 73

5 From pillar to post 93

6 Timepieces 99

7 Show me the way to go home 111

8 Step on it 137

Bibliography 153

Acknowledgements 155

Index 157

'These were the streets my parents knew'

'St Saviours', Aberdeen Park, Highbury, London N.'
John Betjeman, *Selected Poems* (1949)

(*Previous page*) A range of
pieces of street furniture all
carried out in cast iron, c 1895
(*Mary Evans Picture Library*)

Introduction

For me street furniture is any accessory in a street, road or other thoroughfare that is of public use. Even if it commemorates someone, a drinking-fountain qualifies, whereas a monument pure and simple does not.

It might appear from the text and illustrations that this country is still rich in old street furniture, but the examples represent only a fraction of what we once possessed. One has only to compare old prints and photographs with the contemporary scene to realise the full extent of what has gone. By the time you read this many of the remaining examples will have disappeared, victims of decay, obsolescence, neglect, indifference, vandalism, theft and redevelopment.

This is not to say that every piece of street furniture is, *per se*, worth preserving. An undistinguished and irreparable lamp-post or a badly designed, damaged and inoperative drinking-fountain may not warrant keeping. This book, therefore, is not a plea for preservation for preservation's sake. After all, if nothing in this field were ever improved upon, if there were no inventions or discoveries, if there were no new materials, no changes in requirements or in taste, we would still be seeing our way after dark by flaring torches and drinking our water from wells. It would be foolish to retain a lamp-post that costs a large sum to repair or gives insufficient light for modern streets or motorways, and just as silly to keep any piece of street furniture in its original position if it is a danger to traffic or pedestrians. Many pieces, however, have been destroyed for this reason instead of being moved to another, safer site. Although there is something sad and incongruous in seeing a conduit head in a park or a milestone where it no longer is of use, it seems to me better that these should be moved rather than disappear altogether.

Much surviving street furniture survives by accident, because it is off the beaten track, in side roads or alleys, or is too expensive or too difficult to remove altogether or to replace. For the rest, that which we have is what is still useful, well designed, of architectural and historical interest, 'quaint', purely decorative or unusual. I would like to make a plea for us to keep also what is comic, witty or even ridiculous. Few designers in any field today

Plate 1 A street scene, probably taken in the 1920s, showing lamp-posts, lamps on shop fronts, a public lavatory, bollards, gratings and pavement lights (*Council for the Protection of Rural England*)

(let alone this one) have a sense of fun. Must all street furniture be only 'functional', 'tasteful' and 'fit for its purpose'? All these are admirable qualities, but cannot someone design the equivalent of a drinking-fountain that looks like a dolphin or a clock in the shape of a man who lifts his hat on the hour? Why does no one think up a public lavatory that looks like a lion's cage, or make a footscraper in the form of a miniature bull? But perhaps only a confident civilisation, such as the Victorian, can afford the luxury of laughing at itself.

The nineteenth century saw a flood of street furniture. Urban life developed at such a speed that it required not only more street furniture than had previously been needed but new street furniture. Much of this was made possible by the cheapness of (and delight in using) cast iron as opposed to the previously more expensive wrought iron or other materials. *The Smith and Founders' Directory*, a copy-book, was published in 1823 and had gone into several editions by the 1840s. Firms supplying every fitment, from a gutter to a horse trough, proliferated. By the end of the century there were innumerable casting and foundry firms producing huge catalogues. For instance, Macfarlane of Glasgow in the 1880s, on one page of one catalogue alone, showed thirty-four different

'Lanterns for Incandescent Electric Lamps', which could be carried out in tin and copper as well as the ubiquitous cast iron.

It is remarkable that up to about 1830 it seemed almost impossible for anyone to produce a really bad design, and as comparatively few examples of street furniture before this date survive, it is the more important that they be preserved and protected. After 1830 much of what we have is, admittedly, often ostentatious, vulgar and tasteless, but it is never dull. What Victorian and Edwardian design lacks in purity of style is usually made up for in superabundant verve, self-confidence and imagination. After such self-indulgence it was only natural that there should have been a reaction to present-day starkness, when designers have such an aversion to decoration that one feels they regard it as sinful. Perhaps it is time for a swing of the pendulum; human-kind, T.S. Eliot said, cannot bear very much reality, but also cannot live without some kind of decoration—if only by carving its name on trees or park benches or adorning walls with graffiti.

The latter is, of course, a form of vandalism, which is one of the greatest reasons for the disappearance of street furniture. Vandalism has occurred over the centuries but is particularly rife today. In January 1976 teenagers in Coventry flattened no less than fifty bollards in one week, recently all but two of many lovely phantasmagoric roadside benches in Cumbria have been wrecked, few drinking-fountains retain their original iron cups and chains, lamp-post lanterns are smashed, iron railings bent or broken—the list is endless. In 1976 Huntingdon Council thought fit to spend as much as £40,000 on one 'vandal-proof' bus shelter. It was fitted with unbreakable glass, bolted seats and steel fittings all coated with a special material to repel that curse (in the wrong hands) of modern life—the aerosol paint spray.

On the credit side many public and private organisations as well as individuals (from Sir John Betjeman downwards) are now more than ever concerned over the fate of old street furniture. People write letters to newspapers and magazines pointing out the possible destruction of a pillar box or a milestone. When in 1977 the Gas Board wanted to remove 240 gas lamps from Egham in Surrey, there was such an outcry from the residents that the order had to be rescinded. It was decided to preserve, and even have copied if beyond repair, the many gas lamps in the Covent Garden area; and in 1975, when Newcastle Town Moor drinking-fountain was damaged—probably accidentally by contractors laying a new GPO cable—the council had it repaired by their 'very best' mason.

People successfully petition for a horse trough to be filled with plants rather than be destroyed; and they become fond of cabby shelters. Most cities, towns and boroughs have their archivists, architects and planning officers, who keep an eye on street furniture. There are preservation societies, such as the Council for the Protection of Rural England, whose intention is to 'inform, to evaluate, to influence, and if necessary, vigorously to protest' about the removal of country buildings and artefacts. There are local-history societies. In addition, there is the Victorian Society and the Civic Trust in Carlton House Terrace in London, which is concerned with the 'encouragement of higher standards of design'.

Even so, there is little that these worthy organisations can actually do. They have no powers. As a representative of The Royal Commission on the Ancient and Historical Monuments of Scotland put it to me, they can only advise and 'hope for the best'. More often than not recommendations are acted upon, but good as this is, is it really good enough? The Ancient Monuments Branch of the Department of the Environment does have powers, for it can put preservation orders on, repair, maintain, restore, schedule and list any monument that it considers to be of historic or national interest. In the realm of street furniture it is most interested in what almost constitute buildings, such as conduit heads, well houses and hall-type market crosses, but is beginning to include such items as milestones. It is also concerned with preserving old town- and village-scapes in toto, which means the retention of many pieces of street furniture.

Of museums concerned with the preservation of street furniture, the accolade must go to the Castle Museum in York, which houses one of the largest and most comprehensive collections of folk art in the country, opened in 1938. A unique feature is the series of paintstakingly and accurately reconstructed Victorian streets: as well as fully stocked shops, workshops and public houses, there are several examples of street furniture, from a Penfold (c1876) pillar box to a large granite drinking-fountain fitted with a lamp, which was first put up in 1883 at the end of Skeldergate Bridge in the city and removed to the museum in 1961. In June 1976 the Science Museum in London opened a Gas Gallery, outlining the history of this invention, so important for street lighting. Other museums house the odd pieces of street furniture and possess good prints and photographs. Reference libraries all over the country have books and often a good collection of prints, cuttings and photographs. There is The National Monument Library in London and many County Photographic surveys and County Record Offices.

In 1975 the *Daily Express* ran a competition called 'Let's Make a Brighter Britain'. To take part, one had to put a number of environmental points in order of preference, including 'Co-ordination schemes', 'Local eyesore removed or landscaped' and significantly (though referring more to new than old) 'Street furniture made to blend with surroundings'. This question of blending poses a dilemma, for old street furniture often looks incongruous in new surroundings and new out of place in old.

Plate 2 Interesting juxtapositions: in the country —a concrete grit container, iron waste bin, wooden bench, stone stump of an old market cross, a marble drinking-fountain and horse trough. Cledbury Mortimer, Salop (*Geoffrey N. Wright*)

As is explored more fully in various chapters, much of what we still have was not put up without a struggle. Apart from such obvious necessities as wells and conduit heads, other, now taken-for-granted amenities were slow in coming; for the British hate and distrust anything new, and these feelings have delayed the growth and acceptance of other basic needs. Why did it take so long for adequate street lighting, drainage or signposting to be implemented? Granted that invention and discovery had to take place before such things as gas and electric street lighting were available, surely some sort of lighting, some sort of drainage and some sort of signposting could have been possible—as it so often was on the Continent and in America—far earlier than was the case.

Apart from innate conservatism, much of the blame must lie at the door of public and private reluctance to lay out money for the benefit of mankind. One gets the feeling that people preferred to be robbed or raped in the dark rather than spend a penny on even a candle; that they liked earth-closets or a pee in the ditch rather than institute proper drainage or a flush system; that they did not mind not knowing how many miles it was to Babylon, because it was too much bother to put the number on a signpost or a milestone, let alone erect such things in the first place.

As late as the mid-nineteenth century official inertia in the realm of improving a public water supply was a disgrace. A government questionnaire of 1848 asked: 'Have the authorities of the town

Plate 3 Interesting juxtapositions: in the city—iron railing outside a school to prevent children running into the road, cast-iron bollards, pillar box, lamp-posts and an iron drain-inspection cover. Roupell Street, London SW1 (*Author*)

done anything to obtain an abundant and economical supply of water; and are they aware of the advantages of the constant over the intermittent supply?' The response was depressingly in the negative. Brighton Council blatantly answered that it had not even tried; Oxford replied that it never would do anything 'till compelled by parliamentary interposition; Lincoln thought itself 'pure' enough already; and York preferred to spend money on its antiquities rather than on its sanitation. Much of this reactionary attitude was due to the fact that councillors dared not risk losing their positions by adding anything to the rates. The erection of anything from a clock tower to a roadside bench was therefore often left to public subscription, or to the generosity of private people and wealthy and often proselytising bodies such as the Temperance Movement (drinking-fountains) and the Society for the Prevention of Cruelty to Animals (horse troughs).

Despite this conservatism, there is plenty left to see, and I hope that this book will encourage people to be more aware of the old examples of street furniture about them. They cannot avoid looking at buildings, but have they noticed that a church tower carries a one-handed clock or that a public house sports a lamp with its name on it? People may look down a cul-de-sac, but do they appreciate that the bollards that bar the way to traffic are in the shape of cannon or like miniature Gothic spires? When they walk, heads down, do they see that the pavement lights are set in fancy iron surrounds or that the manhole covers carry embossed designs looking like, and almost as varied as, snowflakes? Do they see that this lamp-post is curly and old, and that one straight and modern; that this bracket lamp is plain and new, and that one ornate and probably dating from 1830? Do they notice that a drinking-fountain even if it fails to work, celebrates anyone from a local bigwig to Queen Victoria, or looks like a miniature Indian temple; that stone obelisks are not just a reminder of the ancient world as seen through eighteenth-century eyes but also milestones, the information carried out in beautiful incised lettering?

There are some deliberate omissions in this book. Public-house and shop signs are street furniture but such a large subject that I have, regretfully, come to the conclusion that they would upset the balance of the book. I have left out market crosses, which are too often nearer architecture, and am not sure that stocks and whipping posts qualify as street furniture.

I end this survey about the time of World War I, after which the taste for highly decorated street furniture declined. But artefacts are always changing, and much as one may dislike modern concrete lamp-posts and bollards, litter-bins and parking meters, they are of their period and must be evaluated as such. It is also salutary to realise that in years to come someone will be writing a book registering them and lamenting their passing.

1·Well-watered

Wells

Most people turn on taps connected to a mains water supply in their homes without thinking about it. Though in recent years unaccustomed drought has brought back rationing and standpipes 1.1 the streets to many parts of the country to remind us that not so long ago few people could take mains water for granted. For centuries the only means by which water could be tapped from streams or deep running rivers for public use was through wells, pumps, 'standing' pipes and conduit heads, so that there are still a number of these around. The well is the oldest of such outlets, its importance attested in the British Isles by the many place-names that include the word. Among them are Wells itself in Somerset, Tunbridge Wells in Kent, Wells-next-the-Sea (no longer so) in Norfolk, Well Vale in Lincolnshire, Standwell in Surrey, Whit(white)well in Derbyshire and Shorwell in the Isle of Wight. Among others, Scotland has Langwell in Caithness and Bothwell in Strathclyde; and of those in Wales there is Llandrindod Wells.

In London, Well Walk at Queen Street in the City marks the place where water was available to the public in Roman times. There were sewer wells there between the first and third centuries, and wells were still being dug in the Middle Ages. The Walk itself was given its name about 1677. Other notable Well names in London include Muswell, Sadler's Wells, Camberwell, Chadwell Heath and Clerkenwell. The latter, as its name suggests, was once 'Clerk's Well', dating from about 1180, when, as the chronicler Fitzstephen wrote: 'Around the northern outskirts of London are excellent springs with sweet, fresh, clear water, gushing over glistening pebbles.' Although he may have been using poetic licence, the well was still there in the sixteenth century, when it devolved into a public trough outside Clerken Well Nunnery.

Because of their life-giving properties, wells have long been revered. When the well dedicated to the goddess Coventina at Carrawburh along the Roman Wall was excavated in 1875, many votive offerings such as pearls, safety pins, carvings and more than 16,000 coins were recovered. When Christianity became the official religion, the reverence remained, although the recipient

Plate 4 A typical ancient roadside well with a cross, which makes it a holy place; restored in 1911 to mark the coronation of George V and Queen Mary. Veryan, Cornwall

had altered; as Polwhele in his *History of Cornwall* put it: 'The well before had a spirit; it now had a guardian angel.' Of the many Holywells there is the one in London, which no longer exists in fact; and Holywell in Cambridgeshire, where the covering, topped by a cross, still does.

As the Cornish are among the most superstitious of races, it is not surprising that many holy or wishing wells once abounded in that county, where some are still to be found (Plate 4). As this one, many are cave-like such as that by the road at St Dominick, where the niche for a statue of its patron saint has long been empty; a rough stone edifice in the centre of St Carantocus; and, perhaps the most famous of all Cornish wells, that at St Keyne, with the legend that if a husband drank first, he was the master, but if his wife did, then woe betide him. Many such wells are curiously shaped: for example, the much damaged stone beehive at Digby in Lincolnshire is often mistaken for a lock-up—the name for the small temporary overnight prison still found in many villages and small towns. The Wishing Well at Upway in Dorset is a mere rough round rock with a hole in the middle, but the so-called Robin Hood's Well at Doncaster in South Yorkshire was given its heavy classic stone covering in the eighteenth century by no less an architect than Sir John Vanbrugh, the builder of Blenheim Palace.

As well as being thought holy or capable of granting wishes, many wells were considered to have healing qualities: hence the origin of such spas as Bath, Cheltenham and Tunbridge Wells. There used to be a popular spa at Kilburn, in North London, which was a village in the eighteenth century 'but a morning's walk from the metropolis', as the *Public Advertiser* of 1773 put it. A stone plaque now on Barclay's Bank on the corner of Belsize Road still marks the spot. All that is now left of another popular eighteenth-century spa just outside London is a handful of names—Well Road, Well Walk, Well Passage and Flask Walk in Hampstead. An inscription in Well Walk testifies that healing waters were discovered there in 1698 and that the lady of the manor, mother of the third Earl of Gainsborough, donated the well and surrounding land for the 'sole use, benefit and advantage of the poor of the Parish of Hampstead'. As with so many things, it was not long before the poor were ousted by 'the quality', who turned the well into a fashionable spa complete with Pump and Assembly Rooms, a bowling green and pleasure gardens. The water was so renowned that it was sold all over London in flasks—'the messengers that come for the waters must take care to return the flasks daily'—hence Flask Walk and the present Tavern, which was so named in 1767.

In nearby Fitzjohn's Avenue on the corner of Abenside Road stands a simple (undated) brick and stone pedimented drinking-fountain and dog trough, which was given by one Simon Wimbourren and supplied by the Drinking Fountain and Cattle Trough Association. It was put up for 'the public good' (the public, needless to say, no longer receives this 'good', as no water is supplied). It stands near the site of what the plaque calls an 'ancient' conduit, which was known as 'Shepherd's Well'.

Perhaps the most famous of healing wells still with us is St Winifred's Well at Woolston in Salop. It is said to have miraculously sprung from the ground after the body of St Winifred had rested there for a night in 1138, which automatically gave it curative powers. Now a Tudor 'house' stands over the first of a series of descending stone tanks. Another healing well associated with the same martyr, with the addition of a chapel, is to be found at Holywell in Clwyd. The Holy Well at Malvern, another spa, was held to cure 'many Infirmities, as Kings-evil, Leaprosie, etc' as late as the seventeenth century when the following rhyme was penned:

> A thousand bottles there,
> Were filled weekly,
> And many costrils rare,
> For stomachs sickly;
> Some of them into Kent,
> Some were to London sent,
> Others to Berwick went,
> O praise the Lord.

St Edith's Well at Kemsing in Kent, a low circular brick structure, was held to cure sore eyes, while the Jesus' Well at St Minver in Cornwall was said to be good for all sorts of ailments. St Anne's well at Caversham in Reading is also said to have healing powers, and for this reason was used by pilgrims. In appearance it has seen many vicissitudes, and its present structure dates from only 1908, when it was given a round brick surround topped by an iron cage-like dome, plus an iron cross to denote its religious associations. It was also then fitted with a drinking tap and a pseudo-Georgian shell-shaped basin. But the health-giving Chalybeate water now no longer fills either the well nor does it supply the tap. Nearby recent boring has probably been responsible for changing the water-level overflow, a fate that has befallen many wells and drinking-fountains. About a mile away at Henley Road stands a public house called the 'Flowing Spring', indicative of a fresh-water supply that used to emerge opposite the building but is now threatened by redevelopment.

Wells were, and some still are, favoured by yearly 'Dressings', which was originally a ceremony held to placate the water deity but was soon taken over by the Christian church and 'de-paganised'. Such ceremonies died out when the Puritans had their killjoy say in the seventeenth century but were revived in the eighteenth. Many are carried on today, when the well-head is decorated with designs made out of flower petals, moss and bark etc, pressed into clay. Hymns are sung and the vicar gives his blessing. Derbyshire is particularly noted for such occasions—five wells at Tissington have been regularly blessed since the eighteenth century and the ceremony still takes place to commemorate the escape from a plague at Eyam. The rather elegant stone basin topped by an arch at Dovedale is famous for its Well Dressing, which takes place every Ascension Day.

Most old wells have been considerably altered and are rarely working. The least changed are those still to be found in the gardens of old cottages or on village greens, where they are usually given a wooden and tiled miniature cottage or temple-like covering and called 'well houses'. The well-head near Royston in Hertfordshire is protected by a wooden structure with a slate roof; its 'works' are an elaborate construction of iron wheels. A particularly fine covering can be seen in the village of Aldworth in Berkshire—at 372ft reputedly the deepest well in England. Although no longer in use, its two-tiered tiled roof and wooden columns give it an important air as it stands at the village crossroads. The old well at Fawley Green in Buckinghamshire is a wood and tiled-roof affair, its depth a foot for every day of the year. Like that at Royston its machinery is all large cogs, wheels and ratchets. The old well at Derry Hill in Wiltshire, now converted into a tap, is enclosed in a circular roofed building.

Although off the beaten track, the Rebecca Well on Crazies Hill at Wargrave in Berkshire is worthy of mention. Its little brick building, with a gable and tiled roof, covers the outlet of a spring that used to supply water for the whole neighbourhood. Amid its trees, the little house was put up in 1870 at the cost of £25 by the Rev Grevill Millimore and then named after him. He was responsible for two of the inscriptions, one of which (biblical) reads 'Even by the spring of water shall He guide them', and the other (from Chaucer) 'Take and bless us today, thine are the waters saved from stain'. Later, an anonymous person added another text from the Bible, which gave the well its present name: 'Rebecca and the

Plate 5 The kind of two-troughed well common to the north of England. This one was replaced by a cradle-shaped horse trough in Cradle Well, Jesmond, Tyne and Wear (*Central Library, Newcastle upon Tyne*)

servant of Abraham at the well of Mahor. And the servant ran to meet her and said, Let me, I pray thee, drink a little water of thy pitcher.' Alas, today's Rebeccas would go away with empty pitchers for the well no longer works!

Cradle Well (the well itself, not a place) has the unique distinction of apparently existing in two places at once: on its original site now stands an 1894 horse trough in the shape of a cradle with 'Cradle Well' engraved on it, and some of its stones have probably been re-erected on the site of another well in a nearby park. This well began life as a natural spring, which emerged on the Jesmond Road near Newcastle in Tyne and Wear (Plate 5). As with many such spring-heads in this part of the country it was equipped with a pipe set in a headstone and the water fell into two stone basins, one higher than the other. In this form it only vaguely resembles a cradle, so that the origin of the name is obscure, unexplainable even by oldest inhabitants or local historians. A clue may be found in the fact that the well was on the old pilgrim route to St Mary's Chapel, which stood on the edge of Jesmond Dene (or park) near the Hospital of the Blessed Virgin of Jesmond (considered to be a corruption of 'Jesus' Mount'). Locals still turn 'Lady' (a shortened version of 'Our Lady') into 'ladle', and nearby Hexham's water supply still comes from a source on the moors called Ladle Well. The name might have gone through the following stages: Ladle, Virgin Mary, Our Lady, The Holy Cradle, Cradle Well.

Returning to verifiable fact, we know that in 1903 the old Cradle Well was listed for removal by the local corporation. But a 'neighbouring resident' (as the *Newcastle Daily Chronicle* of the time called her), a Miss Holmes of Wellburn (another well), suggested that as an alternative to destruction the stones be moved to Jesmond Dene. Her idea was taken up by the local Society of Antiquaries and the Parks Committee, which approved of the stones being placed near King John's Well in the Dene, near the ruins of King John's Palace. This well exists and one at least of its basins could be part of the old Cradle Well. For good measure the Cradle Well horse trough stands near a public house of the same name.

Spring water still emerges through troughs in other parts of the country, where the sweetness of the water is preferred to that more easily obtained from a tap. There are two particularly large stone troughs set into the old cobbled street in the small village of Horbling in Lincolnshire. The water comes from nearby Spring Wells and once ran through the street itself; now the course is mostly underground. A fountain in adjacent Fountain Field once supplied water for farmhand and beast, and it was a favourite meeting point for such tired and thirsty workers.

Old wells can come to light during excavations or road-workings. In 1967 in Park Street, Windsor, Berkshire, workmen discovered a well that could be the one recorded in the *Annals of Windsor*. It appears to date from at least 1639, when posts and nails costing £1 7s od were 'sett about' it. A hexagonal brick wall now surrounds the well and its wooden roof is supported by six wooden pillars, the whole mounted on two broad steps, isolated on a wide stretch of pavement. A thick wire mesh prevents anyone from drawing water, or from falling in, but in 1976 the new tap had ceased to work.

Pumps

The pride of all the village is the pump.
The village pump, the village pump,
The village P.U.M.P. PUMP.

This old song emphasises the importance of a form of public water outlet that was easier to work than a well, which is why pumps were both more popular, more numerous, and still with us although many very old ones are now in museums. The lead one that once stood at the corner of Catherine and Milford Streets in Salisbury was put up in 1771, but is now in the city's museum; and there is a 1672 brass pump in London's Barbican Museum. Others are still in situ, even if no longer in working order.

These public pumps or taps, however 'quaint' or 'picturesque' they may seem to us now, were in their time simple necessities. In poor districts one such pump might serve a whole widely scattered neighbourhood. Even so, water was often turned on for as little as only a few minutes a week to 'as much' (the poor were made to feel 'grateful') as 20 minutes a day. An engraving of 1864 shows a pump surrounded by ragged children carrying every sort of utensil. There was so much competition for the precious and grudgingly given liquid that a law actually forbade anyone to carry a club on such occasions. Even water that was piped to houses at this time was turned on for only 8 or 9 hours a week, and the men who worked the stopcocks often had to be bribed to perform their task.

For people in country districts things could be, if possible, even worse. We like to think romantically of the simple and easy country life of the past but even for the gentry, for Jane Austen (who never mentions such 'basics' as a privy or a pump), the necessities of life were often difficult to obtain. In 1840 a public water pipe could be as much as a quarter of a mile away from a house, and even for those accustomed to walking, this was felt to be too far, so that people were prepared to use local muddy and polluted river water for their cooking and washing, fetching piped water only for drinking and for making tea. In 1847 a Miss Ellen Hall was touring the remote mountains of Wales and noted in her diary how the people of Barmouth obtained their water. They had to go to the top of a high hill where there was what might have once been a well but was then a 'horrid, dirty, unwholesome pool of water. Above',

Plate 6 A well kept but unworking wooden pump; its trough filled with earth. The adjacent modern concrete pump with its miserable little tap appears not to be working either. Carsphairn, Dumfries and Galloway, Scotland (*Barbara Denness*)

Miss Hall went on, 'are placed two trough-ways, 'neath which they place their cans and wait about a quarter of an hour whilst each fills with water.' So averse were most local authorities to spending money on making water more easily available, let alone fresh and clean, that even in the whole of England and Wales in 1871 only 3,347 people were employed to cope with the water supply.

The simplest pumps are no more than a serviceable handle and a spout set in a wooden or stone pillar placed over a stone or iron basin (Plate 6). The basin itself was often equipped with a few iron bars on which a bucket or other receptacle could be rested. (On the Continent these bars are still much more in use than in England. In remote villages in southern France I have seen boxes of vegetables resting on such bars in order to receive a good soaking before being sold in the shops or at the market.)

Many British pumps, even if no longer used, are kept in good repair. The tall wooden-posted one in Hutton Henry in Cleveland is maintained by the villagers. The one on the pavement in Rose Street in Cambridge is regularly repainted a sensible black, as is the one from the 1840s in the middle of Queen's Square (off Russell Street) in London (there is a similar one in Bedford Row), which bears the ironic notice that the water is not for drinking. In the market place to the north of the Town Hall in Faversham in Kent there used to be a lead pump that was put up in 1665, when local users were enjoined to 'keep the same in repair'. Either they did not continue to play their part or time played its, for the original has long gone; to be replaced by a sturdy 1869 example topped by a cross. An elegant eighteenth-century wooden pump (now painted blue) in the shape of a simple obelisk still stands at Cornhill in the City of London (Plate 7). It was designed by the architect Nathaniel Wright and erected in 1799 by contributions from the Bank

Plate 7 An elegant, 1799 pump, kept well painted but unworking. Its trough filled with a good crop of ivy. Cornhill, London EC3 (*Author*)

of England, the East India Company and neighbouring fire officers, bankers and traders of the Cornhill Ward. It stands on the site of an old well, which was part of a House of Correction (or prison) built by Henry Wallis, Lord Mayor of London in 1282. Another obelisk-shaped pump is the one at Aldgate, also in the City of London, which is topped by a little stone roof. (It cannot have been good water for the saying 'A draught of Aldgate pump' refers to anything worthless.)

As with wells, many pumps have been given little coverings. The Quay Pump in Paradise Street in Poole in Dorset was given its stone base, wooden frame and pitched roof by the Lord Mayor in 1810. An 'olde worlde' house with gables and a little turret covers the pump in Farmington in Gloucestershire; this house was paid for by an American citizen (who probably hailed from the village) in 1935 to mark the 300th anniversary of the founding of Connecticut. Simpler is the little pump on the village green at Hampton Lucy in Warwickshire, which consists of a metal trough set on stones; the stone pillar holding the spout and handle is topped by an unusual miniature thatched roof.

Other pumps put up by local benefactors include that in the village of Corfe in Dorset, whose rough stone trough has been given a wooden backing carrying the arms of the Bankes family, which held the nearby castle against Cromwell's Army during the Civil War and, so legend has it, only surrendered when a traitor opened the gates. An elegant pump/memorial of 1760 stands in the Market Place at Blandford Forum in Dorset. In stern Classical style, its high pedimented portico and frieze are supported by two Portland stone Doric columns. The inscription carved on a marble plaque tells its story with a flourish and a display of faith so alien to our own prosaic and doubting times:

In REMEMBRANCE of God's Dreadful Visitation by FIRE, which broke out on the 4th June, 1731, and in a few hours reduced, not only the CHURCH, and almost this whole town to Ashes, wherein 14 inhabitants perished, but also, two adjacent villages. And in grateful acknowledgment of the DIVINE MERCY, that has since raised this Town, like the PHOENIX, from its Ashes, to its present beautiful and flourishing State, And to prevent by a timely Supply of Water (with God's blessing) the fatal Consequence of FIRE hereafter; THIS MONUMENT of that dire Disaster, and Provision of the like, is humbly erected by John Bastard, a considerable Sharer in the general Calamity. 1760.

This Mr Bastard, with his brother William and a William Cartwright (all carpenter-mason-builder-architects in the eighteenth-century tradition), were responsible for this edifice, as they were for rebuilding much of the devastated town. John also gave

Plate 8 A Classic-style pump still in working order in about 1920; complete with its iron cups on chains. Most of these have now disappeared from such pumps or drinking-fountains. Buxton, Norfolk (*Author*)

£100 'to keep this pump in repair and supplying the lamp with oil and a man to light the same every night from Michaelmas Day to Lady Day for ever'. Alas, neither his money nor his intention lasted anything like this time! The pump was eventually replaced by a small tap and even the water supply has recently had to be turned off owing to vandalism. The original lamp (an interesting example of early street lighting) has now been replaced by an ugly little collection of electric light bulbs that look so much at variance with the elegance of the structure that it would be better, one feels, for it to be left unlit, if that is the best that the local authority can do.

Mention of a light over this pump brings us to the fact that many pumps (and other public water supplies) were supplied with lighting. Apart from the old oil lamps, one of the earliest gas ones must be that illustrated in a *London Directory* of 1827, as put up by the 'Cast Iron and Pump Founders & Engineers' G. Turner & Son of 63 Dorset Street off Salisbury Square. Their lamp topped an obelisk-shaped pump, and one very like it still stands in the Market Place in Southwold in Suffolk. This was put up at the expense of G. E. Child and carries the town arms, which consist of a dolphin and an arrow-pierced crown; not unnaturally a dolphin forms the water-spout, and the iron lamp is supported by two more dolphins.

There used to be another obelisk-style pump with a gas lamp on the top outside the police station in Soho in London. Augustus Pugin, that most uncompromising of medievalists, used an illustration of it in his *Contrasts, or a Parallel Between Noble Edifices of the 14 and 15 cents and similar buildings of the present day; shewing The Present Decay of Taste*, a pamphlet published in 1846. Pugin so hated the prevailing taste for Classic (he was responsible for the Gothic decoration of the Houses of Parliament, built between 1839 and 1860) that he called such buildings as the National Gallery, the British Museum and All Souls, Langham Place, a 'national disgrace'. He naturally used this, admittedly not very attractive, Classic-style pump as a contrast to the 'better' over-elaborate Gothic conduit of 1479 that used to stand at West Cheap.

Although not in the street, a typically lamp-topped pump stands in a stone-flagged square on the green of Durham College in County Durham (Plate 9). It is a plain wooden column and the lamp is of the wall-bracket variety. Another example can be seen in the Market Place of Faringdon in Oxfordshire, where an elegant twisty two-branched iron lamp stands atop of what looks like a much older stone pump or drinking fountain. Preservation-

Plate 9 This exceptionally tall wooden pump carries an equally exceptionally large bracket lamp. Buckets or other containers were balanced on the iron grid, College Green, Durham City, County Durham (*Barbara Denness*)

conscious old Hemel Hempstead in Hertfordshire boasts a fine iron pump, which was erected by public subscription in 1848 and carries a contemporary, or probably later, lamp. The pump in Dorchester, Dorset, was put up in 1784 over a well on the site of the old Market House, and, in addition to being encased in a stone pillar, carries a light standard.

A series of identical iron pumps lines the route between Allendale and Catton in Northumberland. This part of the country is, or rather was, rich in lead-mines, the lead being brought by horse transport through Hexham, Riding Mill and other places, to be shipped, and these pumps provided refreshment for man and beast. Each pump consists of a Classic-style column with a dome and finial; and the water-spout is in the form of a lion's head— a favourite device for many a pump or drinking-fountain. The basins of these pumps were provided with an iron grid and an iron cup on a chain, but few of the former are intact or the latter still there.

Although most are no longer working and in a sad state of repair, they represent a rare example of nineteenth-century planning—planning that came out of necessity and not from a remote architect's or designer's drawing board. They are either set in rather grand niches (Plate 10) or now stand forlornly on village greens or roadsides. In 1975 the one at Acomb, which even lacks its finial, was propped against a stone fountain and horse trough in the middle of the road. These pumps were made by Glenfield & Co of Kilmarnock in Scotland in the 1870s and 1880s, and this firm supplied the same design for other parts of the country. An unused lopsided one stands on the grass verge near the bridge in the pretty 'unspoiled' village of Castle Combe in Wiltshire, and the same design can be seen—and this one still works—at Ticknall in Derbyshire, where it was erected on 18 April 1874. A rather more decorated version with a few 'Classic' acanthus leaves at its base is to be found on the village green at Watton-at-Stone in Hertfordshire. This has been given an elaborate temple-like covering: wooden columns, slate roof and a little turret topped by a ball. A similar pump at Latimer, on the Buckingham/Hertfordshire border, also stands on the green, and its 'temple' has a pagoda-like roof covered in curved tiles.

Not all pumps supplied water for either humans or animals. For many centuries roads were often impassably muddy in winter or over-dusty in summer. Nothing much could be done about the former state, but those who could afford it (and it was rarely the local authority or the government) could do something about the latter. One such benefactor was Beau Nash, of Bath fame, who for his own and his visitors' comfort in 1754 paid for a series of pumps to be put up along the road from London to Bath. They comprised tall wooden columns with a high handle and spout. Outriders

Plate 10 One of the series of pumps put up between Allendale and Catton in Northumberland for the main use of lead-carrying carts—for man and beast. The cup has vanished and the water no longer flows from the lion's mouth. The pump was put up by the Pelican Band of Mercy on 5 January 1889 and is therefore a gesture by the Temperance Movement. Newbrough, Northumberland (*Barbara Denness*)

went ahead of coaches and horsemen and used these pumps to dampen dusty roads. One of these examples of private enterprise can still be seen near London Airport at Poyle in Berkshire.

Such pumps or 'standing pipes' were also used along some coast roads for the same purpose, as they were conveniently near available sea water, thus saving the use of horse-drawn water-sprinkler carts, which needed to make a longer (and more expensive) journey to obtain supplies of rain water. Just off the pier at Clacton-on-Sea in Essex one can still see a post that marks the spot of an old sea-water inlet tap; from here a gas engine piped water to pumps along this part of the coast.

Conduit Heads

An English satirical broadsheet of the late sixteenth century called *Tittle-Tattle; Or, the several Branches of Gossiping* shows the many places at which women spent their time in this all-too-human and pleasurable activity; among them were the Church, the Market, the 'Alle Hous' and the 'Conditte'. At the last, women are shown chatting while queueing to fill jugs and buckets from an elegant round building, in the Classic style, which covers the public water supply.

These 'heads' are more sophisticated and often older coverings for water outlets than pumps, and, being usually elaborate and sometimes quite large, often rank as architecture. Few of them remain. They became necessary in large towns when many wells became unusable owing to pollution, the water being obtained from outlying districts and drawn through pipes to emerge through taps covered by these decorative edifices. But being in towns they eventually became traffic hazards and were destroyed or moved.

Conduit heads appeared in London as early as the thirteenth century, but these exist now only as street names. The last one in London, the 'Chimney' or 'Devil's Conduit' in Bloomsbury, was demolished in the eighteenth century by the Duke of Bedford, who owned much of the district, and the stones were removed at his expense. One of the most important was the Roundhead Conduit— not, as might be imagined, named after one of the combatants in the seventeenth-century Civil War but put up in the fifteenth century and deriving its name from the fact that it was conical in shape with a sphere on the top. It was fed by water from gravel beds in Bayswater (hence Conduit Place there), and was situated in Conduit Fields, which, in its turn, in 1713 became Conduit Street, now running between Regent Street and Bond Street. It supplied water until about 1840, when more up-to-date provisions were made. This Roundhead pipe ran along Oxford Street as far as a spring near the Tyburn river, where, at Stratford Place, it joined an even older conduit belonging to the City of London, and supplied water for this area.

Then there is White Conduit Street, to which water was conveyed from a medieval spring in Pentonville; and Lamb's Conduit Street, where an Elizabethan dam trapped water in a reservoir with water from one of the tributaries of the old Fleet river.

All that is left of Leicester's once proud conduit is a photograph, some drawings, a print and a slate tablet telling its story: 'This Conduit was first founded by M. Eliz Orpwood Anno 1612. Rebuilt in ye year 1709. James Annis, Mayor, Edward Palmer, Francis Coltman Chamb.' Much the size of a summerhouse, it was an octagonal structure, and once stood in the Market Place, its lead cistern receiving water through lead pipes from St Margaret's Spring outside the town. It was considered to give particularly good water and was very popular for the making of tea, which arrived in this country in 1652. It was even more popular, one assumes, when, at the time of public rejoicings, it ran with ale or wine for 'the benefit of the lower classes, which crowded round and struggled for the filling of their jugs and cans'. It was demolished and rebuilt about 1847 and 5 years later transferred to the farmstead of Abington Wigstone, where in 1950 it was housing a pedigree bull calf. By this time it was a shadow of its former glory, much of its brickwork having gone. By 1952 the farm had been turned into Abington School, which had no use (and apparently no respect) for such a useless relic. Moves were made to have it transferred to Leicester Museum, but as it was only a copy and so dilapidated, even this institution refused to house the remains.

Such street furniture not so much vanishes as, like old soldiers, merely fades away. Two instances can be cited from Bristol in Avon. Here the Old Quay Pipe has been moved around so much that now all that is left of it are some fittings in the possession of the Bristol Water Company. When it was erected in what is now Clare Street in 1534, it boasted ornate castellations and a head of Monus, the god of laughter, water (or perhaps the occasional wine or ale) being understandably considered a happy liquid. In 1717 it was moved nearer the river, and in 1770 its stone canopy was destroyed and a fountain and horse trough put up in its place at the then Tontine Warehouse near the harbour. A tablet on the wall at the junction of St Stephen's and Colston Avenue, marking the spot, reads: 'This tablet, erected in 1973, marks the last site of the Quay Pipe Conduit, which for many years was one of the principal sources of water supply for the inhabitants of the city and for ships in the harbour.'

Bristol's Temple Pipe has as interesting and as sad a history. It was first built as early as 1366, its water supply coming from Raven's Well at Totterdown. It was owned by Sir John de Gourney, who was granted permission to make it available to the public. The pipe ran from the Friary near Temple Gate, but in the seventeenth century was extended as far as Temple Street—hence the name of the pipe. During the late sixteenth century it was given a statue of Neptune; by tradition this is said to symbolise the defeat of the 1588 Armada but it is more likely that it was only an obvious emblem to put over a water supply in a port. Alterations were made to this conduit head in 1785, when it was moved to a lane near the Temple Churchyard. It was moved again in 1892, this time converted into a drinking-fountain, to the junction of Temple and Victoria Streets. In 1949 it was cleaned and repaired when the authorities, showing some respect for even a much altered piece of a minor ancient monument, finally re-erected it at the Bridgehead in the centre of the city.

The fact that this conduit once carried a statue of Neptune brings us to another example. In Wharton Park, overlooking the railway station at Durham, stands a larger than life lead statue of this god, now damaged and propped up, on a strange funeral pyre of stones. It looks, perhaps longingly and regretfully, towards the

Plate 11 This elegant conduit was built c1830, although, as the over-life-size lead statue of Neptune was made in 1792, it could be earlier (*Durham County Record Office*)

Market Place, where it was a prominent and well loved landmark for over 190 years.

Its various peregrinations make one of the most interesting of transformation stories concerning old sources of public water supply. The story begins in 1450, when water was pumped to some sort of outlet in the Market Place, but it is not until 1831 that we have pictorial evidence of a conduit head (Plate 11). We do know that the lead figure of Neptune was made in 1792, so that the

Plate 12 This photograph, taken c1860, shows the conduit to have been, in reality, less tall and narrow than the artist had depicted it (plate 11). Also, by then, it was in a state of disrepair and probably no longer in use (*Durham County Record Office*)

conduit itself may well date from then or indeed earlier. This statue is said to have symbolised the hopes of eighteenth-century Durham merchants (vain, as it turned out) that the River Wear could be made navigable to Durham and thus link it to the sea for foreign trade. Whether or not the conduit was still in working order when the photograph (Plate 12) was taken in c1860, it certainly appears to have become neglected. It is interesting to note that the photograph gives the lie to the early nineteenth-century artist's engraving, which made the structure much taller and more elegant than it really was. (One suspects that many buildings and artefacts of which there is now no more than contemporary drawn evidence may be wrongly depicted.) What is certain is that by 1844, when the City Water Company was formed, the conduit was no longer the city's main water supply.

By 1863 the Victorian Gothic Revival was at its height and the then old-fashioned eighteenth-century building was thought 'unsightly'. Although grudgingly admitted to be 'venerable' and 'a prominent feature' of the 'ornamentation' of the Market Place, it was callously demolished and replaced by a fountain of such full-blown Gothic design as to have met the full approval of such medievalists as Pugin and Ruskin. It was even given matching Gothic lamp-posts. It still retained its earlier Neptune, but not without some opposition. Among local followers of Messrs Pugin and Ruskin were those who considered it pagan and outdated, but when they saw it repainted and regilded, they had to agree that it added to the fountain's appearance, although with typical Victorian Philistine eclecticism they did not appreciate the incongruity.

This new fountain had not been put up with unanimous approval. The *Durham Directory* was glad to report that after a long series of council discussions the fountain was at last a 'substantial reality'. Substantial indeed! The reporter, not being endowed with an original pen, called it a 'Thing of Beauty' which he hoped would remain 'a joy for ever'.

As the public, who were conservative and probably anxious to keep a well known landmark, however useless and unkempt, failed to subscribe enough money for a replacement, the sum was taken out of the rates. The result was nothing if not biblically symbolic. Sculptured discs showed Hagar 'Athirst in the wilderness'; Moses striking the rock; and, over the cattle trough, a representation of Jacob at the well, with the text: 'Drink and I will give thy camels drink also.' The Victorians obviously saw nothing comic in the possibility of such beasts appearing in an English market place.

The *Durham Directory's* reporter had to admit (and here one agrees with him) that it was by no means an easy task to convey in words any idea of the 'actual whole'. He did his best; indeed his full description, once he had recovered from his initial reticence, is too long and tedious to quote in full. Enough to learn that he thought it 'elegant' and 'graceful', that (Neptune apart) it was 14ft high and made of Prudham stone embellished with Aberdeen and Peterhead granite. In his summing-up the reporter called the fountain-cum-trough a 'kind of classic-Gothic—Gothic in spirit and detail; classic in its severe and simple lines'.

It did not, needless to say, fulfil the reporter's poetic hopes. 'For ever' lasted as long as 1900, when yet another change of artistic taste decreed that Victorian Revival Gothic was in its turn 'unsightly'. Official taste, in the main, having reverted to the Classic, the new conduit was a cumbersome edifice, which, with its Doric columns, dome and odd crown-like cornice—still topped by the ubiquitous and more appropriate Neptune—seemed made to last. But even this was not to be. In 1923 it was pulled down, at a cost of £79. Nothing replaced it, for the days of conduits or drinking-fountains, however 'venerable', were over. But even the authorities could not bring themselves to destroy Neptune; hence his dignified preservation in Wharton Park.

Many pumps and conduit heads have been moved from their original positions, either because they were obsolete or got in the way of new roads and increasing traffic. Cambridge's Hobson's Conduit, originally put up at Market Hall, now stands on the corner of Lensfield Street, having been moved to this site and re-erected by public subscription in 1855. It is an elegant Jacobean design, which was reconditioned and its Royal Coat of Arms painted in 1967, when a plaque, put up by the Hobson's Conduit Trustees, was unveiled by the lord mayor. Thomas Hobson was a local carrier whose strange habit of allowing anyone to hire only the first horse available, irrespective of worth, instituted the saying 'Hobson's Choice'. As well as being a noted carrier, he was a great benefactor to the town, and when he died in 1630, he left an estate for the maintenance of the conduit that now bears his name. From Milton he received what must be one of the nicest epitaphs, whose last couplet goes:

> If any ask for him; it shall be said,
> Hobson has supped, and newly gone to bed.

In 1788 Oxford's Carfax conduit was removed 5 miles outside the city to a slope on the grounds of Nuneham Park. Its name is an English corruption of the French *Quatre voies* or four ways, which arose from the fact that the conduit was at first buit at a crossroads. It was put up in 1610 'to the great content of the inhabitants of Oxon', and Clerk Wood in his *City of Oxford* of 1661-6 called it 'very faire and beautifull . . . such for its images of ancient kings about it, gilding, and exquisite carving, the like (except probably in London) not to be found in England'. It was given by Otho Nicholson, an examiner of the Chancery and a diplomat and courtier who was trying to curry favour with James I. It cost him nearly £2,200, plus the £100 he left in his will for its maintenance, though this sum was never used for the purpose, but 'juggled away', as often happens to such bequests. The water came from the hill above North Hinksey, whence it was carried by a large lead pipe through various outlying districts to a great cistern within the conduit, and thence into other cisterns and by 'divers other great pipes' to 'severall colleges and sundry privat houses'.

A 12ft-square stone building, decorated with arches and topped by an elaborate Gothic-style pinnacle it was designed by John Clark, a courtier. The 'ancient kings' mentioned by Wood included James I, King David and Andaticus, King of the Lepides, there were also the emperor Charlemagne and the 'worthies' Hector of Troy and Godfrey of Bouillon (a noted Crusader). It also carried the arms of English royal houses back to Henry VIII as well as those of the University and the founder. Statues of the Four Cardinal Virtues (Justice, Temperance, Fortitude and Prudence or Wisdom) stood above the arches, and there were also 'various ornaments, as boys, obelisks, flowers and fruitage interchangably transposed on all four sides'.

The most striking feature was a large representation, 'carved by a good hand', of Queen Maud riding an ox—a reference to the city's name of Ox-ford. At the time it was put up no one would have been shocked by the fact that the 'good and wholesom' water issued from the animal's penis or that wine flowed from the same source on 'extraordinary days of rejoycing'.

When it was erected, there was plenty of room around it, but 50 years later it was already being considered a danger to traffic, the street having become narrower and more congested. It was not, however, until 1788 that it was taken to pieces and reassembled on its present site. For a long while this splendid example of Jacobean allegory and heraldry suffered the ravages of time and theft, many a king, worthy or ornament finding its way into private hands. In the late 1950s a proposal by the Department of the Environment to have it returned to Oxford was abandoned as being too costly, and for a time even restoration was delayed. This has now been carried out, all its statues and etceteras having been faithfully copied and restored (they have even added a portrait head of the architect responsible for this work!) but the ox has not, the Department now having some doubts that it ever existed, despite the fact that it appears in early engravings.

Gloucester's Scriven's Conduit is now to be found in Hillfield Garden, a public park half a mile outside the town, where its late Gothic arches perform the sensible function of a summerhouse. In 1634 it was put up in Gloucester itself in Southgate Street by an ironmonger, the water coming from Mattes Knoll, which is traditionally known as Robin Hood's Hill. In its new function it is now unconnected with any water supply, weathering and superficial damage having much harmed it. Its numerous resitings—in 1774, 1830 and finally in 1938—have not exactly improved its appearance.

Chelmsford's first water supply was piped across the fields from Burgess Well to a conduit head outside the Shire Hall, where the Tindal statue now stands. In 1814 a small round temple was put up and later in the century it was given a wrought-iron frame topped by a street lamp (Plate 13). It stayed thus until 1940, when

Plate 13 Chelmsford's fine 1814 conduit photographed in the 1890s when it still stood on its original site in the High Street. Now, minus its lamp, it has been removed to nearby Tower Gardens (*Chelmsford County Record Office*)

it became an obstacle to increasing traffic, and it has now ended up—minus its ironwork and lamp—a useless folly in local Tower Gardens.

Edinburgh can still boast two out of its four original square Classic conduit heads topped with urns. One stands near Midlothian County Hall, the other near John Knox's house in the High Street in the old part of the city.

A sombre 1597 conduit head still stands on its original site in the corner of the Market Place in Grantham in Lincolnshire. As early as 1314 water from springs in the nearby fields of Gonerby was conveyed by pipes to the Friary of Grey Friars of Grange in Grantham. About the time of the Dissolution of the Monasteries in the 1530s the pipes were extended to a reservoir in the Market Place, after which the present structure was erected. At the end of the seventeenth century the Grange was still privately owned by a Robert Fysher, but in 1684 the corporation obtained from him a grant of free and 'perpetual' use of the water, undertaking to keep both the conduit pipes and 'house' in good repair. It needed this repair in 1793 and again in 1927, when the modern obelisk-shaped pinnacles were added. It is not certain when the pair of drinking-fountains was attached; in the ubiquitous form of lions' heads they are topped by elegant carved stone ribbons. Unfortunately the repair does not now extend to these fountains, as they are no longer in working order; even the original iron cups on their chains having vanished. The conduit ceased to be the town's main water supply when the Water Works were constructed in 1850, the water coming from other sources than Gonerby.

Many drinking-fountains now stand on the sites of old conduit heads. The ornate eighteenth-century fountain in the Market Place in Wells in Somerset was put up in 1798 to replace a medieval conduit head—an arched structure given by a resident bishop. Southampton used to have four conduit heads, but these were replaced by drinking fountains in the early nineteenth century.

2· A sound of coolness in the busy street

Drinking-fountains

The Norman-style public drinking-fountain set into the railings surrounding St Sepulchre's church at Holborn Viaduct in London was put up in 1859. It is unusual among such fountains nowadays in that it still carries its original iron cups on chains, its (now modern) tap actually works, and its brass work is kept shining bright.

This may be because it was the first of such fountains to be put up in London, and immediately inspired the many others still to be found all over the country. For this reason 21 April 1859, when this fountain was declared 'open', is an important date for such amenities. The ceremony was one of those mixtures of solemnity, piety and snobbery at which the Victorians so excelled (Plate 14) It was an occasion that needed the irony of a Dickens to record, but we have to make do with the prosaic account given by an anony-

Plate 14 The well attended 1859 opening ceremony of London's first public drinking-fountain, outside St Sepulchre's church at what is now Holborn Viaduct. Mrs Wilson (daughter of the then Archbishop of Canterbury), the guest of honour, is seen taking the first sip of water from a special silver goblet (*Illustrated London News* 1859)

mous reporter of the *Illustrated London News*. Failing the Archbishop of Canterbury himself, his daughter, Mrs Wilson, was the guest of honour. Along with the other notables, she made her way in a procession from the church to the fountain, where the vicar made a long speech.

He pointed out that, as they were in the shadow of his church, he had been deputed to place in Mrs Wilson's hands a silver goblet 'that you may take the first draught from the first drinking-fountain erected in this metropolis'. He reminded Mrs Wilson that she was not committing herself to a 'mere experiment', still less to one of 'doubtful result', because, although it was the first such London fountain, it was not by any means the first in the country; Liverpool, Hull and Derby were among those that already had their 'fountains of refreshment for the people', the success of which had exceeded the 'most sanguine expectations'.

The vicar then told his listeners that The Metropolitan Drinking Fountain Association, in which the Archbishop had taken a deep interest, had already been formed 'for the purpose of extending the benefit of this service throughout the metropolis'. This Association had been given £500 by Mr Gurney, the generous presenter of the fountain in question. 'And I doubt not', went on the vicar, 'that under the auspices of this institution, with the blessing of God, there will be, in due time, no considerable interval in a walk through the streets of London where the weary and thirsty passenger may not be refreshed by a draught from some such fountain as this of pure and wholesome water.' Here he was honest enough to admit that this benefit was not for such as himself or Mrs Wilson—let alone the Archbishop of Canterbury—gentlemen and ladies all, who would never have been in the position of being weary and thirsty passengers on foot, but for the lower classes or, as the vicar put it: 'the poor and hard-working portion of the people'.

Here he mentioned another strong reason for the installation of such a benefit: the Temperance Movement. (Of which more later.) The vicar hoped that 'intemperance, with its attendant miseries' would be alleviated by the 'moral' help of such fountains. It was indeed (he admitted) for this very purpose that this fountain had been erected; it was committed to the (intemperate) poor for their safe keeping. They were to 'preserve [it] inviolate', so that it might be a 'blessing to them and those who may come after them'. At this point he presented the tastefully bonneted Mrs Wilson with the silver goblet, which he hoped she would have the goodness to accept. Doing her duty, Mrs Wilson took a sip and declared the water to be excellent.

There were further speeches. Mr Wakefield, the president of the Association, echoed the hope that this fountain would be only one of the first of such and that 'pure water might prove in every respect as beneficial as it must always be agreeable'. Failing royalty, no such ceremony was complete without a member of the aristocracy, and this one was honoured by the presence of Lord Radstock, who, on behalf of the Association, was requested to declare the fountain open. He did not beat about the bush—nor would even those of this audience who fell within this category have expected him to do so—when he also pointed out that the fountain was for the special use of the working classes.

After this short admonition Mr Wakefield again took the platform and thanked the donor, Mr Gurney, for having 'solicited' the honour of Mrs Wilson's presence. Making further references to the future, he pointed out that as there were few blank walls other than churches in the metropolis suitable for such fountains, it was on these that future examples were expected to be placed. He thought it 'impossible to devise anything more appropriate than thus to connect this simplest act of charity intended for the relief of the poorest classes with these our most ancient ecclesiastical edifices'. With this the 'proceedings . . . terminated', and Mrs Wilson, with the other VIPs, repaired to the Vicarage for (one imagines or hopes) something stronger than 'pure water'.

Although moved further along the wall when the Viaduct was built in 1867 and lacking its outer arch, the fountain looks much as it did when Mrs Wilson performed her little duty. The reporter on the *Illustrated London News* described the fountain in full:

> In a recess hewn out of the churchyard wall two small pillars are fixed, from the top of which springs a semi-circular arch, neatly moulded; the side of the recess, with the arch itself, are of polished Aberdeen granite. In the centre is a tastefully-wrought shell of white marble, also highly polished.

As well as the words 'The first drinking-fountain' and the name of the donor, it carried the instruction 'Replace the cup' and the words 'Filtered from the New River Company'. This 'new' company was by then 246 years old, and it was only wound up in 1904, when the Metropolitan Water Board took over the task of supplying London's public water supply.

In 1859 Mr Gurney was also responsible for a similar fountain erected behind the Royal Exchange. When the Association reached its Golden Jubilee in 1909, it was decided to celebrate this achievement by replacing this fountain with a much grander affair, which was finished 2 years later and presented to the Corporation of the City of London. (It stands very near the Cornhill pump.) It is a temple of a fountain in reddish marble and bronze, which shelters a bronze, lightly clad female pouring water from a pitcher into four marble basins (Plate 15). The water still flows and there is even one cup on its chain. The statue very much resembles that on

Plate 15 The 1911 temple fountain which was put up to celebrate the 1909 Golden Jubilee of the Metropolitan Drinking-Fountain and Cattle Trough Association. In reddish marble and bronze it shelters a classical female from whose pitcher water still flows into four basins, although only one original cup remains. Behind the Royal Exchange in London EC4 (*Author*)

a fountain (merely on a plinth without a covering) which the indefatigable Mr Gurney caused to be put up on the north side of Blackfriars Bridge in 1861.

The Metropolitan Drinking Fountain Association's hopes were amply fulfilled. On the very evening of the inauguration at St Sepulchre's a meeting of the St Martin-in-the-Fields vestry voted unanimously to erect a drinking-fountain at Charing Cross. This fountain no longer exists; the only one still in this vicinity is that fixed to the surrounding wall at the rear of the church at the bottom of Adelaide Street. It was put up in 1886 as a memorial to William Gilson Humphrey, BD, scholar and divine, who was vicar of the parish from 1855. A simple granite round-arched affair, it bears a strong resemblance to its parent at St Sepulchre's, and although no longer working, its brass fitments are kept brightly polished. Also resembling the original is the one given by Marmaduke Langdale in 1859, which is still in the wall at Endell Street in Soho; but water no longer flows from its stone shell and the whole thing is sadly neglected. At the time of writing the wall was due for demolition, so that the fountain may well have gone by the time this book is published.

The new London fountain also inspired the Islington vestry committee to decide to remove the police station on its Green and replace it by a drinking-fountain! This was a curious decision, as one would have thought a police station the more important; it must have been a very small station or a particularly large fountain. Another fountain, now standing in a wall outside St George's Hospital in London, was built in eighteenth-century style with a 'rococo' shell basin, though it was put up in 1861.

The rest of the country soon followed suit. A drinking-fountain was erected near the Sally Port in Chatham, Brighton council asked for designs to be submitted to it, and a fountain for Southampton was already in process of erection in 1859. The Coventry Board of Health agreed to the proposal put forward by the city's United Temperance Society that a fountain be erected, the Society being prepared to spend £5 a year towards the water supply. Scarborough was not slow; neither was Sunderland, which put up three fountains at important points in the town. Oldham erected a fountain in polished Aberdeen granite (a favoured material), which was paid for by the King Street and Werneth Co-operative Society. The mayor of Handley in Cheshire announced his intention of celebrating his 1859 year of office by giving the town a 'particularly beautiful' drinking-fountain.

But perhaps the grandest of all such artefacts of this period is the Dudley Fountain in Dudley, West Midlands. As well as being far larger and more elaborate than the London 'first', it was declared open with such pomp and circumstance as to put St Sepulchre's little ceremony in the shade. The fountain was the gift of the Earl of Dudley, and the opening ceremony took place on 17 October 1867. The 28ft high edifice, vying in magnificence with the fountains of Rome, was placed in the middle of the Market Square on the site of the old Town Hall. It is still there and still dwarfing its surroundings, only a few seats and flower beds having marked the passage of time.

The fountain was designed by James Forsyth in the form of a triumphal arch in heroic Italian Renaissance style. Decorative water gushed from the mouths of two enormous sea-horses and from a four-tiered fountain under the arch; and drinking water spurted from two dolphins into troughs for horses and from two lions' heads for humans. The pair of female classic deities that top the whole carry a whole harvest festival decoration on their heads. One cannot blame the *Art Journal* of the time for finding the fountain impossible to describe; although a local writer, full of civic pride, called it the finest drinking-fountain in the United Kingdom, and the *Illustrated London News* gave the opening ceremony full coverage, with no hint of criticism.

It was an occasion worthy of royalty. Not only was the square decorated with flags on poles but it was also lined by mounted members of the Worcestershire Yeomanry Cavalry with drawn swords. These had escorted the procession of dignitaries, which included the Earl and his Countess, Lord Lyttelton, the vicar, magistrates, the corporation of the borough, borough officers, carefully selected visitors, the proud sculptor (who was also responsible for the Perseus Fountain at Witley Court) and a deputation from the local temperance society. Owing to illness, the mayor missed this landmark in the town's history, his place being taken by his deputy. When all were assembled, the Vicar of Dudley offered up a prayer and his lordship expressed his hope that his gift would be found as useful as it was beautiful. The deputy mayor gave his thanks on behalf of the people of Dudley; the president of the temperance society added thanks and Lord Lyttelton spoke for the county. These formalities over, Mr Forsyth had the honour of drawing the first glass of water, which was given to the Countess in a goblet 'of chaste and classical design', ornamented with an engraving of the fountain. After an obligatory sip, the Countess declared the fountain open and the property of the people of Dudley. She, like her husband, hoped that the fountain had a career of usefulness in store.

Later, however, when horse traffic declined, the water for the troughs was turned off and some people wanted the fountain moved to another site. It therefore suffered a period of neglect, but during the borough's centenary celebrations of 1965 it was cleaned and the water turned on again, except for the horse troughs, which, in line with so many others, were converted into flower beds.

Why this sudden proliferation of public drinking-fountains? One reason was that by this time many town and village pumps had been stopped up, either because of the impurity of the water, which caused the then prevalent cholera attacks, or because of the introduction of low-level sewers. Another reason was that, at long last, local authorities were realising that it was their duty to provide an adequate and efficient public water supply. But one of the main reasons has already been hinted at—the influence of the Temperance Movement. This dedicated, powerful and wealthy organisation quickly realised that public drinking-fountains were an easy and obvious way of extending their influence. As Benjamin Scott put it: 'I one day saw in Cornhill eight or ten people waiting at the pump there to drink; and it struck me that fountains or pumps in the streets would save men from drunkenness.' The Movement seems, however, not to have appreciated (to paraphrase a proverb) that you can take an alcoholic to a fountain but you cannot make him drink.

Thomas Whittaker (1813–99) was the first man to devote his life to advocating total abstinence, and during his lifetime the Movement grew and grew. There is no doubt that the over-drinking of alcohol was a very serious problem in the nineteenth century. A leading figure in the Temperance Movement called it the 'master-curse of the day . . . a national crime and a national disgrace of the first magnitude'. From the 1850s onwards most support for The Cause came from the middle and lower-middle classes and those respectable artisans who were enfranchised in 1867. These people came especially from such nonconformist strongholds as the North of England, Wales, the West Country and East Anglia. The 'United

Plate 16 The flamboyant drinking-fountain memorial to Sir Wilfred Lawson, Bart (1829–1906), the great champion of the Temperance Movement which was responsible for so many of our drinking-fountains. This one is disproportionately large for the small town in which it stands, Aspatria, Cumbria (*Barbara Denness*)

Kingdom Alliance' was formed in 1853 with the avowed object of suppressing the 'Liquor-Trade by the operative will of the people' —an admirable but rather naïve hope. The titles of similar alliances and societies have a fine (if often smug) ring to them: the 'Central Sunday Closing Association', 'Friends Temperance Union', 'Original Grand Order Total Abstinence Union' and the 'Women's Total Abstinence Union'.

The Movement's most dedicated fighter was the baronet Sir Wilfred Lawson (1829–1906), who devoted much of his life in and out of Parliament to The Cause. It is therefore very appropriate that the memorial put up to him in his home town of Aspatria in Cumbria should have taken the form of a drinking-fountain (Plate 16). A Renaissance-style structure, it is topped by a St George who is (presumably) killing the Dragon of Liquor. It also carries a bas-relief portrait of the Great Man. (Recently an irreverent and, perhaps, inebriated wag stuck a cigarette between the disapproving lips.) The inscription, worthy of that on some Westminster Abbey monument, reads as follows:

Remember Sir Wilfred Lawson, 2nd Baronet of Brayton and Isel, in whose honour this fountain was erected by his many friends and admirers. Beloved for the Integrity of his Life and the Height of his Ideals, an Example for all Time of one who gave Himself for Others, believing in the Brotherhood of Man. A Lover of Truth and Mercy, a Brave and Strenuous Advocate of Temperance and Peace, which sacred Causes he championed in the House of Commons for forty years, with Gay Wisdom and Perseverance.

Many other fountains bear witness to the zeal of the reformers. In 1861 the Bath Temperance Society, founded in 1836, paid for a fountain to be put up outside Bath Abbey. It carries a fairly common and obvious statue: that of a scantily clad female pouring water from a pitcher, often referred to as 'Rebecca at the Well' (Plate 17). Alas, this particular pitcher is broken and water no longer flows into the basins. There is now only a small modern tap. The fountain carries a favourite temperance inscription: 'Water is Best'. Another example carrying the same words is the large dark red stone fountain in the Renaissance style in Newcastle, which was erected in 1894 by the Band of Hope (a branch of the Temperance Movement) near the cathedral, but was subsequently moved to Bigg Market. Its position is appropriate, as it somewhat resembles a market cross and its steps are used as a communal resting place in the time-honoured fashion of such crosses. The fountain no longer works, but there are many 'wicked' public houses around to cater more substantially for the thirsty on market days.

Newcastle can boast an even grander temperance-inspired

Plate 17 A 'Rebecca at the Well' fountain erected in 1861 by the Bath Temperance Society, proudly proclaiming the virtue of water over all other liquids. The pitcher is broken and no water flows into the basin. Outside the Abbey, Bath, Avon (*Geoffrey N. Wright*)

Plate 18 A fine example of full-blown Edwardian 'Classic' style, this fountain memorial to W. D. Stevens was erected by public subscription in 1901. It no longer works. Clayton Road Corner, Newcastle, Tyne and Wear (*Barbara Denness*)

fountain. It stands at Clayton Road Corner and is in Edwardian heavy-classic style, with an arched pediment, obelisks, swags and the protection of little railings (Plate 18). It was put up in 1901 to the memory of W. D. Stevens, 'A Citizen of Lofty Ideals and Strenuous Endeavour'. This fountain/memorial was paid for out of public subscription (it must have cost a bomb) 'in Recognition of the Open-Hearted Charity, Activity, and Unfailing Geniality' of Stevens, who, although he was president of organisations that promoted marine commerce, is important to this book through his 'Association with the Cause of Temperance'. Unfortunately the fountain is now minus its tap, so that the healthful free water no longer flows for the 'Betterment of the Poor and Needy'.

The fact that this is a memorial brings us to another reason why so many public drinking-fountains were put up during the nineteenth and early twentieth centuries. It was realised that a memorial, to a public or private person, could serve the dual purpose of providing free water. As such, a considerable amount of

Plate 19 This red terracotta and marble drinking-fountain with bronze details was put up on the frontage of Drury Lane Theatre in London to commemorate the great impresario, Sir Augustus Harris (1851–96). Oddly, it bears no date or inscription. It is now sadly neglected and much obscured by modern street signs (*Author*)

money was often spent, which is why so many of these fountains are disproportionately large for the villages they 'grace'.

One of the most imposing of fountain/memorials in London is that put up to Sir Augustus Harris (1851–96), the great Drury Lane Theatre impresario (Plate 19). As he held such sway there, and was responsible for some of the grandest pantomimes of the period as well as encouraging Continental players and was himself part-author of many melodramas, it is only fitting that his monument is placed against the front wall of the theatre. Oddly enough, it bears only his name and the words 'Erected by Public Subscription'—no date or overblown inscription. In Renaissance style, it is made of red terracotta and rough and polished marble, and embellished with bronze Cupids and musical instruments. The whole thing is sadly chipped and neglected, the tap no longer works and its ample basin is usually filled with rubbish—a disgrace to the memory of an important man and the important building against which it stands.

Almost as grand is a stone fountain (again in Renaissance-style) put up to the memory of Henry Fawcett in 1886, which stands in the Victoria Gardens on the Embankment in London. It is also equipped with an ample basin, the water-spout in the form of a well-modelled dolphin. The water used to be obtained by pushing a button, and could be drunk from two large bronze cups on chains, which have now gone. It carries a bas-relief portrait of the blind Liberal politician and economist, and is dedicated to him by his grateful country*women*, perhaps because his wife, Millicent Garrett Fawcett (1847–1929), was an ardent suffragette and one of the founders of Newnham College, Cambridge.

A lonely yet welcome drinking-fountain, plus horse and dog troughs, stands on the roadside beside Grasmere in the Lake District (Plate 20). The simple Norman-style structure, with its steeply pitched roof, rough masonry and spare carving, blend in well with the landscape, making it a rare example of thoughtful design. It was put up in 1889 as an aid to travellers and a memorial to Lakeland's greatest poet, William Wordsworth, a verse from whose series of sonnets 'Personal Talk' is carved on one side.

Plate 20 In contrast, a simple 'Norman' drinking-fountain, horse and dog trough which was erected in 1889 to the memory of William Wordsworth (1770–1850). By the side of Grasmere in the Lake District (*Barbara Denness*)

Many Americans have returned to these shores to trace or visit their forbears' homes but few have left behind them a gift in the form of a drinking-fountain and horse trough. This public-spirited idea came to one Alexander Cook of Chicago, who visited his native town of Egremont in Cumbria in 1904. The fountain is, unfortunately, rather ugly. Mr Cook would probably have been hurt to know that future generations saw fit to remove the tap, and even he cannot have foreseen that there would soon be few horses left in the street to take advantage of the trough. Only dogs can remain grateful: that is, if there is ever any water in their basin.

Appropriately the memorial to Captain Matthew Webb is given a water connotation in the form of a drinking-fountain, as he was the first man to swim the English Channel, in 1875. The fountain/memorial was put up in Dawley, Salop, where he was born in 1848, and stands in the library forecourt; it was put up in 1900, though he had died in 1883 at, of all places, Niagara Falls. It takes the form

Plate 21 An elegant 1888 drinking-fountain on the sea-front at Cullercoats in Tyne and Wear. It was erected to honour Lieutenant Adamson who had perished on HMS *Wasp* the previous year (*Barbara Denness*)

of a vaguely Classic obelisk, each side equipped with four basins and lion-head spouts. A fountain/memorial to a sailor also has a certain appropriateness, especially as it is on the sea-front of Cullercoats in Northumberland (Plate 21). The site was given by the Duke of Northumberland in 1888 to enable 'a few friends' to erect a fountain to the memory of Bryan John Hythwaite Adamson, Lieutenant RN, who had lost his life while serving queen and country on HMS *Wasp*, his ship having sailed from Singapore in September 1887 never to be seen again. The elegant Victorian Gothic fountain carries the Lieutenant's cipher and flying wasps; for one whose name literally was 'writ in water' it is sad that this liquid no longer flows from the four lion-head spouts.

Of a service nature but on a more happy note is a fountain that was put up on Southsea Common, Portsmouth, in 1861, the farewell gift of Major-General Sir James Yorks Scarlett, CD, to the people of Portsmouth and the garrison, of which he was the retiring commander. It no longer exists, but it was obelisk-shaped, its four corners adorned with bronze dolphins that spouted water into shell-shaped bronze basins. The sides carried the arms of the borough and those of the general. It was topped by a glass globe street lamp, which at night (as a contemporary account put it) 'lit up the gushing waters' and added 'novelty'. An innovation was the fact that the water was carried from the town waterworks in patent bituminised pipes, which were considered to be more durable than the usual iron ones.

Much too large for the pretty village it adorns is a Jacobean-style stone fountain in Corsham in Wiltshire. Perhaps it was built in this manner to echo nearby Corsham Court, the home of Lord Methuen. The unworking edifice is, oddly, undated. It was erected by the inhabitants of Corsham and district in memory of C. M. Mayo, CC, 'as a token of respect for his services to this parish during many years residence'. The horse trough is planted with flowers.

The tragic South African or Boer War of 1899–1902, which so saddened Queen Victoria's last years and tarnished Britain's image throughout the world, inspired its quota of memorial/fountains, one of which stands proudly on the village green in Bellingham in Northumberland. Mounted on broad stone steps, the column carries the figure of a soldier who stands, rifle reversed, under a canopy topped by a fallen hero's wreath. The water basins remain, but the taps have gone. There is a rather Gothic-style example in the same county, at Allendale, with an urn instead of a soldier; it was put up to the memory of John Joseph Glendinning of the 14th Squadron, Imperial Yeomanry, who 'lost his life in the service of his country at Klip Drift, South Africa, on March 7th 1902'.

The whole of the British Isles, as well as past and present countries in what was the Empire and is now the Commonwealth, is littered with memorials to Queen Victoria. Many of them celebrate her Golden Jubilee of 1887 and her Diamond Jubilee of 1897 in the form of drinking-fountains. Of those in the London area, one can single out the red marble fountain that stands at the top of Shaftesbury Avenue where it joins New Oxford Street. It was put up to commemorate the 1897 Jubilee by the Board of Works for the St Giles district, and is heavily Romanesque in style. Its original taps and cups have been removed and replaced by two modern taps, only one of which was working at the time of writing.

A magnificent (or ugly) 1887 market cross of a monument/fountain stands in the broad crossroads in the middle of Jedburgh in Roxburgh (now Borders) in Scotland. As well as displaying bas-relief plaques of the monarch and now defunct taps, it carries four elaborate brackets for electric lights—which are also not working. An 1897 example at Lee near Chesham in Buckinghamshire is a six-sided affair with a tiled roof. A Frances Elizabeth Ellis paid for a very simple stone fountain of 'pure water' to be erected at White Waltham in Berkshire to commemorate her monarch's 60 years on the throne. A print of 1834 of the Market Place in Hexham in Northumberland shows an elegant stone pump with a large and serviceable trough. This has now been replaced by a red stone affair called the 'Temperley Memorial Fountain', a tall column in the Renaissance taste and in summer nicely hung with baskets of flowers. An Art Nouveau panel declares that it was put up 'for the Common Good . . . Near the Site of the Old Market Pant [drinking-fountain] in the 60th Year of the Reign of Queen Victoria and the First of King Edward VII AD 1901.' It is remarkable for also carrying a rather long poem written by a local versifier, Wilson Gibson, who was only twenty-three when he penned it:

> O you who drink my cooling waters clear,
> Forget not the far hills from whence they flow,
> Where ever fen and moorland, year by year,
> Spring, summer, autumn, winter, come and go,
> With showering rain and storm and snow.
> When over the green bents forever blow
> The four free winds of heaven: where time falls
> In solitary places, calm and slow,
> Where pipes the curlew and the plover calls,
> Beneath an open sky my waters spring
> Beneath the clear sky welling air and sweet
> A draught of coolness for your throat to bring,
> A sound of coolness in the busy street.

Ironic words, as water no longer sounds or cools.

On a lower social scale but touching in their thoughts are the many drinking-fountains put up by ordinary people in memory of ordinary people. Such a one stands in the little 'park' at the end of West End Lane in London NW6. A simple marble obelisk, it was put up in 1897 by Miss Miles in memory of her mother, who had lived in the district for 76 years. Miss Miles thoughtfully provided a basin for dogs, but this kindness is now no more extended to them than it is to humans.

The bas-relief of a horse's head set in an 'Elizabethan' cartouche would appear more suitable for a horse trough than a drinking-fountain, until one learns from the inscription that it was put up by the friends of Robert Fisher 'as a memorial of the high esteem in which he was held, as a general townsman and a fine sportsman, who was devoted to horses'. Unworking, it now stands in the quietness of Castle Park in Whitehaven in Cumbria, having originally stood in Tangier Street, whence it was moved in 1911. Of a like nature, although this one is still in situ and works, is a drinking-fountain in Jesmond Road in Newcastle. In rather heavily conceived marble, it includes a horse trough; it was put up in 1895 by the widow of William Long 'in affectionate remembrance of his lifelong interest in and kindness to dumb animals'.

A fine fountain of almost 'Eleanor Cross' proportions—although more Classic than Gothic—was erected by George Moore (not the writer but a local philanthropist) in memory of his wife, who died in 1872 in Wigton in Cumbria. Its four bas-reliefs, which depict Acts of Mercy, were executed by Thomas Woolner and have been praised by Nicholas Pevsner. Unfortunately one act of mercy, that of providing free water, no longer operates, as all the taps and basins are blocked. Much more neglected is the odd pant that stands on the village green at Staindrop in County Durham. It looks as if it were made up of fragments of Gothic churches and even has a spire, but its much neglected unworking state is an insult to the generosity of Lady Augusta Mary Pouletter, who, in May 1865, gave it to the parish in memory of Sophia, Duchess of Cleveland, whose coronet and cypher it bears.

Some early fountains-cum-pumps seem to have been made out of bits and pieces of old buildings. For example, the one on the village green at Bamburgh in Northumberland (Plate 22) appears to have been constructed out of fragments of a medieval, or at least a Gothic Revival, church. Its four-sided turret is pierced with pointed arches, and, with its little roof, it perches uncertainly on a disproportionately small stone base. The metal lion-head spout, even if it worked, would now only water the flowers that a thoughtful local council has planted in the stone trough beneath. Locals would call this fountain a 'pant', this being the word for such an object throughout most of the north of England. The origin of the word is obscure. *Chambers Dictionary* admits this, but defines it as meaning a puddle or midden. Cecil Greeson in his *Northumberland*

Plate 22 A curious 'pant' or North Country drinking-fountain and pump which appears to have been made out of fragments of a church. Bamburgh, Northumberland (*Barbara Denness*)

and Durham Word Book calls it an old northern name for a fountain, and cites examples to prove that it was in use from 1593. In his *Glossary of North Country Words* John Brockett gives the word the same meaning and supports Skinner (another linguistic authority) in maintaining that pond was originally pronounced 'pand', which in its turn may have derived from the Saxon 'pydam', which means to enclose or shut up.

Two other Gothic remnants or Gothic-style pants in the same county are worth describing. The one at Riding Mill looks like something out of a 'Gothick' novel: set into a stone wall under a pointed arch, it consists of only a simple basin (complete with iron bars), a lion-head spout, and over this a vaguely medieval stone shield carrying an elaborate cypher and the date 1873. If all such edifices were so helpful as to carry dates, the task of historians and archaeologists would be so much easier. With knowledge one can date most objects within a few years by their style, execution and condition, but with so much 'revivaling' having gone on, one can sometimes be misled. A case in point is the Gothic-style pant put up to the memory of Miss Evelyn Lowrey in Hexham in Northumberland. It appears to be late Victorian or Edwardian Gothic, but it was in fact put up between 1932 and 1934, the monumental mason responsible for the work having taken the design from an old book.

There is a particularly fanciful and interesting pair of cast-iron pants, in County Durham and Cumbria. They were made by Glenfield & Kennedy of Kilmarnock in Scotland, who were prolific manufacturers of all kinds of ironwork. These pants look like miniature pavilions or canopies in a happy (or unhappy) mixture of Indian, Gothic and Classic styles. One, in Middleton-in-

Plate 23 This singularly ornate covering for a simple pump, in Indian/Gothic/ Classic style, is painted dark green. It was presented in 1879 to the Corporation of Sunderland by the Oddfellows in memory of one of its members. Nenthead, Cumbria (*Barbara Denness*)

Teesdale, is the better kept of the two and has, as a centrepiece, the figure of a boy sitting on a dolphin mounted on an elaborate pedestal. It has quite recently been given a new water-spout, and the whole thing is imaginatively painted in cream, black, orange, yellow and dark blue. For some inexplicable reason the undersides of the arches are decorated with little models of crocodiles, which have been painted a jolly bright red, reminding one of the reptiles that cavort so wickedly in Walt Disney's 'Dance of the Hours' sequence in his *Fantasia*. This fountain was erected by R. W. Bainbridge of nearby Middleton House, and the following inscription is repeated on all four sides: 'In commemoration of a testimonial presented to him and Mrs Bainbridge by the employees of the London Lead Company and other friends, Sept 28, 1877.' The identical covering can be found about 25 miles away in the village of Nenthead in Cumbria on the second pant. It is painted dark green but lacks the boy on his dolphin, and instead has a broken and unworking pedestal pump (Plate 23). It carries the same inscription, which is explained by the fact that the operations of Mr Bainbridge's lead company extended over this area—the lead being taken down the Tyne Valley to Blaydon (from the German *Blei* for lead), where it was put on boats destined for London and abroad.

Plate 24 Even more ornate and even more an amalgam of styles, this pump covering carries a representation of an early steam engine, 'The Royal George', which was made in 1827. The covering itself was put up in 1914. Shildon, County Durham (*Barbara Denness*)

This sort of canopy seems to have been popular in this part of the country, as another (not quite so ornate) example, its design leaning rather more to the East, is to be found at Mowbray Park in Sunderland in Tyne and Wear. It was also made by Glenfield & Kennedy, and its centre (unworking) tap is mounted on a ribbed and domed column. It was presented in 1878 to the Corporation of Sunderland by the Oddfellows MU in memory of one of its members, and for some strange reason carries the words 'Keep Dry'. Again with a strong Eastern feel to it, and particularly ornate, is another at Shildon in the same county (Plate 24). Of special interest to railway enthusiasts alternate plaques show embossed representations of one of the earliest of steam engines, the 'Royal George', which was constructed in 1827 by Timothy Hackworth, a friend and colleague of George Stephenson, creator of the famous 'Rocket' locomotive. The 'Royal George' was made at the Shildon works and is locally and loyally considered to be superior to anything built by Stephenson. The fountain was presented to the inhabitants of Shildon by the members of the Old Shildon Workmen's Club in November 1914.

This part of northern England is rich in drinking-fountains, many of them put up before London's first official one in 1859. Most of them, however, are in poor condition. A simple pedimented urn-topped stone slab still stands against a wall in Hencotes, its iron spout rusty and its elegantly fluted basin usually filled with rubbish. On the grass verge at St John Lee stands a Roman temple of a pant, with a rounded arch and a fine urn; but its bowl is broken and its spout dry. Equally tomb-like is a heavy stone pant dated 1858, which stands at Tanner's Row in Hexham; its four sides are pedimented and its iron works sadly out of order. In the battle of the styles, Classic v Gothic, which raged throughout the nineteenth century, this part of England seems to have come down heavily in favour of the Classic, for yet another 1859 iron pant set in a rough stone wall in Lowther Street in Whitehaven in Cumbria is also in this style. Its lion-head spout no longer ejects water into its simple basin, which, along with the dog trough, has its quota of detritus, the town's arms on a shield above only serving as a reminder of the council's neglect.

Looking as if it might have been made in the eighteenth century is the Roman-tomb-like fountain set in a wall in the one-street village of Whalton in Northumberland. It is elegant and simple, the work of a man who clearly knew his Classical onions, until one looks closer and realises that it also carries a pair of incongruous medieval bosses. One is therefore not surprised to learn that it was put up as late as 1911.

Also Classic—a simple marble pediment mounted on a block of stone—is a fountain that was put up in 1859 on a wall of the East Gate in Warwick. This brings us to the subject of wall-fountains, which vary considerably in size and in the material used to make them. One of the simplest (perhaps because some of it is missing) is the stone one on the clock tower at Creetown in Kirkcudbright-shire (now Dumfries and Galloway) in Scotland. All that is now left of this fountain is a granite basin, and above it a panel bare of any decoration; at one time there must have been a spout and at least one cup on a chain. This area is also quite rich in wall-fountains. Much more ornate—again on a clock tower, which is part of a gatehouse—is one that was put up in 1883 at Fleet. It has a fine spirited phantasmagoric dash to it, as a stone scallop enfolds a gargoyle-like head; its basin also has a scallop enclosed by what looks like a pair of human arms (Plate 25). It carries a quotation from the 104th Psalm: 'He sendeth the springs into the valleys, which run among the hills.' Although the Deity may still send these springs, man has long since done his part in providing an outlet—a case indeed of God proposing and Man disposing.

Plate 25 A remarkably exotic and decorative Rococo-style drinking-fountain basin which was given by Mrs Murray Stewart in 1883. She also gave a horse trough which stood beneath it but which has now disappeared. Nor does any water flow from the gargoyle-like head. On the clock-tower, Gatehouse of Fleet, Dumfries and Galloway, Scotland (*Barbara Denness*)

There is a lovely green-earthenware Art Nouveau fountain (c1900) fitted to a wall beside the railway station-house in Alston in Cumbria. Its rounded back is decorated with a relief of what look like corn-on-the-cob plants. There is now a nasty hole where the spout used to be, and it bears the unequivocal (if now in-accurate) word 'Water'.

A very simple marble wall-fountain can be seen in a little grotto in Richmond Park in London. It was put up in 1887 and carries the following rather ambiguous verse:

> Here quench your thirst
> And mark in me
> My emblem of true charity,
> Who while my bounty I bestow,
> Am neither seen nor heard to flow.

The words are only too apt, as the water is neither seen nor heard. This fountain was equipped with Maigen's *Filtre Rapide* to protect the drinker from the ill-effects of excessive calcium.

In an age obsessed with, and often justifiably proud of, its cast-iron work it is not surprising to find this material forming not only the working parts of drinking-fountains but also the whole struc-ture. Many were free-standing columns fitted with as many as four cups on chains, and often with a dog trough, and carried out in a riot of every known (and unknown) architectural style. There were also grand affairs adorned with lilies and swans and set on wide plinths. Cast-iron wall-fountains were often made in the form of a column with an iron backing, such as the one illustrated in MacFarlane's Castings' (Saracen Foundry, Glasgow) catalogue, which carries the injunction to 'keep the pavement dry'. This catalogue also shows many elaborate wall varieties, such as a water-spout set in a shell-like niche surrounded by an excrescence of jumbled decoration. The blurb beginning a section (in the 7th, 1904 edition) devoted to 'Fountains for Streets, Squares, Roads, Parks, Gardens, Schools' etcetera is worth quoting in full for its information and period flavour:

A supply of drinking water to the outdoor population, and also to the lower animals, is now an acknowledged necessity of the changed circumstances of the times and the growing intelligence of the community, encouraging habits of temperance and humanity, and promoting the moral and physical improvement of the people. The appliances in this Section will be found well adapted to this end. We call particular attention to the simple action of our Drinking Fountain Supply Valve. By pressing the lip of the drinking cup against the valve stud as shown in the illustrations, the water flows into it, the operation being thus performed by one hand only.

Plate 26 All that 'Water for the Thirsty' on this stone and iron drinking-fountain has done is to disfigure it with rust which no-one has seen fit to remove. In a grand 'fire-place' design, it was put up in 1866 in Darlington, County Durham (*Barbara Denness*)

What the optimistic Victorians and Edwardians had not fore-seen, however, was that of all materials cast-iron is the most susceptible to rust, which is why so many iron examples from this period are now in so sorry a state. As few local authorities nowadays seem to think it worth while to clean them, they have become more often eyesores than interesting decorative historical adjuncts to our streets and parks. There is such a one in Darlington, County Durham—a cast-iron fountain set in a Classic-cum-Gothic stone surround. With its iron part in near-Renaissance style and an arch supported by pillars decorated with trophies, it is an interesting example of Victorian eclecticism, but rust now disfigures the area below which the water used to flow (Plate 26). Carrying the now ironic message 'Water for the Thirsty' it is dated 1866 and called a

'Hygienic Spa Drinking Fountain'—the last thing it is now! In an even more sorry state is the smaller iron example in Creetown (Dumfries and Galloway), which is in a simple 'fireplace' shape, decorated in (fairly) accurate Norman style, and set in a rough stone arch. Its surface and grill on the pavement are in a disgusting state of rust, and its injunction to 'Praise God from whom all Blessings Flow' is now only a piece of blasphemy.

Some drinking-fountains carry what appear to be particularly incongruous decorations—until one learns the reason. The finely sculptured stone wild boar that sits on top of a simple two-tapped (working) drinking-fountain at Ripley in North Yorkshire seems to have no meaning until one learns from the inscription that it was the gift in 1907 of the Hon Alicia Margaret, Dame Ingilby, whose family crest is a boar. Another family emblem more usually found on a fountain is the superbly rendered dolphin-like fish with a tap in its mouth, as in the village of Cambo in Northumberland,

Plate 27 This dolphin drinking-fountain is one of the supporters of the coat of arms of the Trevelyan family one of whose members paid for it to be sculpted between 1880 and 1886. The family motto: 'Not unmindful of future generations', carved upon it, is apt, as the whole thing still works. Cambo, Northumberland (*Barbara Denness*)

where it is one of the supports of the coat of arms of the Trevelyan family. It was put up by Sir Charles Trevelyan between 1880 and 1886; and the family motto, 'Not unmindful of future generations', inscribed in Latin on the stone, is particularly apt, as the tap works and the original cup is still on its chain (Plate 27).

Cattle, Horse and Dog Troughs

Although one can accuse some of those responsible for drinking-fountains of having ulterior motives, such as encouraging temperance among the lower classes, the same accusation cannot be levelled against those who urged the provision of water for animals in the streets. For centuries animals had had to make do with rivers, ponds, streams or water provided in buckets by their owners, and it was not until the early nineteenth century that people began to feel that animals were important enough to have special provision made for them. There is a print showing a horse making use of a primitive wooden trough that was erected by the Clapham and Streatham and Brixton Society for the Prevention of Cruelty to Animals; now, although this print bears no date, it cannot have been executed before 1824, this being the year when the RSPCA was founded. It was at first called the Animal Protection Society, becoming 'Royal' in 1840. Judging by the horse-owner's clothes, the print was probably made in the 1830s and carries the caption: 'Cheap practical benevolence, worthy of imitation.'

This benevolence was indeed eventually found worthy of much imitation. By 1867 another influential body began to add its weight to the growing altruistic concern for thirsty pets and 'beasts of burden'. This was the already mentioned Metropolitan Drinking Fountain Association, and at this date its committee announced that 'at the urgent request of many of their supporters, they have henceforth resolved to make the erection and maintenance of drinking-troughs for horses, dogs, sheep, and oxen, a more prominent feature of their work'. In consequence of this request being accepted the Association added 'and Cattle-Trough' to its title, so that any such trough bearing this name cannot have been put up before 1867. One has to remember that cattle were a not uncommon sight in London even at this date. In 1837, the year when Queen Victoria ascended the throne, sheep still grazed in St James's Park, a fact supported by the 1867 committee, whose members were worried about 'the intense suffering' experienced by all kinds of animals from thirst in the city of London.

By this date the Association was already responsible for fourteen troughs in London, and the number of human fountains with troughs attached amounted to 110.

An engraving (locality unspecified) in the *Graphic* of 1876 shows no fewer than seven horses from carts or Hansom cabs taking advantage of a long wooden trough, while a fashionable woman allows her dog to drink from the lower trough provided for smaller animals. Being so subject to decay, most of these wooden troughs have long disappeared, surviving ones being made out of stone, granite, marble or iron. Most of the round iron ones have gone, but there is still an unusual stone trough (now filled with earth) in Little Venice in London's Maida Vale. Although by the early 1900s the motorcar was beginning to oust horse traffic, the old troughs were still very much used and still made in some quantity. Macfarlane's was only one of the many firms manufacturing them and its catalogues show a number of shapes and sizes, many fitted with a drinking-fountain with cups so that horse and rider could quench their thirst at the same time (Plate 28). Some of the iron ones were given traditional lions' feet (such as were popular on household baths at the time); others, more appropriately, are supported by horses' legs and hooves, such as that still on the grass verge on the Harwich road in Essex.

Among the stone troughs that have gone one must count the elegant example, complete with human drinking-fountain and

Plate 28 A man and horses benefit from a grand and ornate iron fountain. Macfarlanes, who could provide it (with lantern if required), considered it 'the least possible obstruction to traffic'. Alas, this sort of obstruction has finally sealed the fate of many such fountains. C1885 (*Mary Evans Picture Library*)

Plate 29 Now gone—modern public lavatories in its place—is this stone pillar of a lamp-post with fine lamp, horse trough and drinking-fountains. It was photographed at the turn of the century shortly before its destruction in 1908. George Street, Richmond, Greater London (*Libraries Department, London Borough of Richmond upon Thames*)

topped by a lamp, which used to stand in George Street in Richmond, Greater London (Plate 29), and much resembled the Aldgate pump. It was removed in 1908 to make way for the underground public lavatories that now occupy the site.

As with drinking-fountains, many troughs were also memorials, like the grey marble example (with a drinking-fountain) in Carlton Hill in London NW8 (Plate 30). It was put up by the Metropolitan Association and bears the simple inscription 'In Memoriam, J. S. L. A. 1888'. An iron plate carries an interesting warning: 'The water supplied is the property of the Association and is for drinking purposes for man and beast. Persons using the water for other purposes will be prosecuted.' One can only assume that people found the large trough suitable for washing either their clothes or themselves! A very simple trough in Hopton Street in Southwark in London bears a surprising inscription to the memory of Charles Kingsley, who died in 1875. One would have thought a fanciful fountain more appropriate to the author of *The Water Babies*. Another memorial trough is the granite one in Penzance in Cornwall (Plate 31), which carries the following touching inscription:

'In memory of Little Simon Bolitho who passed this way 1905 to 1910.'

The classic simplicity of these examples is fairly common; some were even simpler, being merely long bath-like cast-iron objects that could be supplied 'with or without self-acting supply apparatus'. As with drinking-fountains, troughs were often engraved with biblical quotations, the most popular being 'A righteous man regardeth the life of his beast' (Proverbs XII, v 10). The now plant-filled stone trough next to the War Memorial in the High Street in Canterbury, Kent, carries the following inscription:

To our patient comrades of the Horse lines,
He paweth in the valley, he rejoyceth in his strength.

'Horse lines' refers to the fact that during World War I horses were greatly used on the battlefield, and suffered as many casualties as the men.

Plate 30 The rather crude basic design of most horse troughs (this also has a small tap for humans) which was put up by the Cattle Trough Association in 1888. It is now rubble-filled, neglected and dirty although others are sensibly plant-filled. Carlton Hill, Maida Vale, London NW8 (*Author*)

Plate 31 In contrast, this well designed granite trough was put up in 1910 in memory of five year old Simon Bolitho who must have been fond of horses. Penzance, Cornwall (*Robert Enever*)

3. Convenient

It would not be difficult to appoint a patron saint of public lavatories. The halo would undoubtedly go to George Jennings, the Victorian pioneer, to whom all those in this country who have ever been 'caught out' must be eternally grateful. An appropriate place at which to erect a chapel in his name would be the underground convenience (part of the tube station), at the Royal Exchange in London. Here Jennings put up the first such public loo, though unfortunately this historic construction no longer exists, the present one dating from 1911.

It was the culmination of a long struggle, not only by Jennings but by others over the centuries. Not so with the Romans, however, who were great ones for sanitation and probably the first in the field. In AD 315 there were 1,444 public latrines in Rome and one for every twenty-eight people in Timguid. This service was provided all over the Empire. London was well off, and Houseteads on Hadrian's Wall in Northumberland had a latrine 31ft by 16ft, which consisted of a long trough that may have been fitted with seats.

As with so many other things Roman, these marks of civilisation almost disappeared in the Dark Ages. In 1291 there was a 'common privy' at the head of Phillips Lane in London Wall, within Cripplegate Ward, and at about the same time a 'four-holes' (four-seater) with a roof was put up at Temple Pier, south of Fleet Street, over the Thames. Although not so ancient—it is presumed to be 200 years old—there is still a six-seater at the Manor House in the village of Chilthorne Domer in Somerset, in a building made of rubble walls with a stone-tiled pyramid-shaped roof. There are four adult-sized and two child-sized seats with lids, let into benches on three wooden-panelled walls. In 1973 the Department of the Environment gave £135 towards its repair, £600 having already been spent on its preservation.

To retrace our steps, in the fourteenth century there was an average of only one public latrine for each of London's wards. The one at Ludgate, soon after its construction, was found to be defective, 'perilous' and the cause of 'grete disease'—which must have been a gross understatement. Despite the fact that Elizabeth I had the first indoor flushing privy installed for her use at Richmond

Palace in the sixteenth century, public facilities were still a rarity. It was not until the middle of the nineteenth century that a few people began to wake up to the idea that an adequate sewerage system was needed. In 1849 the editor of *The Builder* wrote 'Sewers are in and it is high time they were', but latrines themselves were far from 'in'. In the 1850s Edwin Chadwick, the great sanitary reformer, battled against the usual obstacles of vested interest and prejudice, and did much to promote a better system.

It is here that George Jennings comes upon the scene. He made a plea for 'conveniences suited to this advanced stage of civilisation' in place of 'those plague spots that are offensive to the eye and a reproach to the Metropolis'. He went on to say: 'My offer (I blush to record it) was declined by Gentlemen (influenced by English delicacy of feeling) who preferred that the Daughters and Wives of Englishmen should encounter at every corner, sights so disgusting to every sense, and the general public suffer pain and often permanent injury rather than permit the construction of that shelter and privacy now common in every City in the World.' The opposition was so great that Jennings remarked caustically that those against his proposal could never have been 'in need' themselves. He also maintained that 'although my proposition may be startling I am convinced that the day will come when Halting Stations [as they were rather coyly called] replete with every convenience will be constructed in all localities were numbers assemble.'

In 1851 the Great Exhibition was held in the revolutionary new Crystal Palace in Hyde Park. Here was a 'locality' indeed where great numbers assembled, and Jennings saw his opportunity. Despite opposition, he was allowed to install conveniences where people were charged a penny a head—hence the euphemism 'to spend a penny'. The next year the 1st Duke of Wellington died and was given a sumptuous funeral at St Paul's; one witness, Lady Stanley, was as much impressed by the fact that 200 of Mr Jennings' conveniences were provided for ladies. She wrote to her daughter-in-law: 'How the world improves!' It was an optimistic view, for a report only two years later made no apology for publishing facts about the scarcity of public latrines, pointing out that everyone must be aware of 'the suffering endured by all, but especially by females, on account of the want of them'. Even when the Crystal Palace was re-erected at Sydenham in 1855, the installing of public conveniences there was opposed as being too costly. One 'wit' asserted that 'persons would not come to Sydenham to wash their hands'—yet another typically English euphemism. But Jennings won the day, and his lavatories eventually brought in £1,000 a year.

It was not until the 1870s, however, that Jennings' dream became more or less a reality. Alas, few from this era survive. Although, when one looks at illustrations of the most primitive, it is perhaps just as well. The most basic, called 'ordure closets' (a name which has a nice honest eighteenth-century ring to it), were often just long iron troughs that could be plain, painted, galvanised or enamelled, but lacked a single seat. Better ones were fitted with hinged wooden seats, and better still were those with a low partition between the seats. Such communal latrines, ordure closets or what-have-you, must have given ample opportunities for indecent goings-on, and here we must touch on one reason for the disappearance of a number of old public lavatories. Many, especially the free-standing or against-the-wall iron or brick men's standing-only lavatories have for long been the haunt of homosexuals, who use them not only for picking-up places but for illicit activity. When such lavatories become particularly notorious, the police close them or have them pulled down. It is said that when one of the famous small round pissoirs in Paris (hated by Madame de Gaulle) was removed for this reason, a regular 'patron' laid a wreath on the blank spot.

Plate 32 One of Bristol's three magnificent 'temples of convenience'. These round 'Gentlemen's' are now very rare. C1870–80, Horfield Common, Bristol, Avon (*Geoffrey N. Wright*)

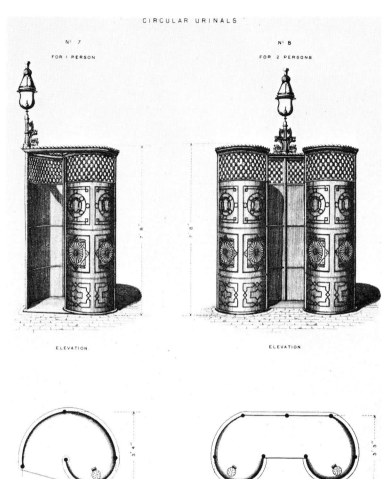

Nº 7

FOR 1 PERSON

Nº 8

FOR 2 PERSONS

ELEVATION

ELEVATION

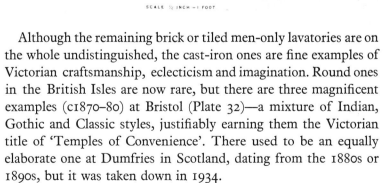

PLAN

PLAN

SCALE ½ INCH = 1 FOOT

Plate 33 Designs for circular urinals, complete with lamps, 1881 (*Mansell Collection*)

Although the remaining brick or tiled men-only lavatories are on the whole undistinguished, the cast-iron ones are fine examples of Victorian craftsmanship, eclecticism and imagination. Round ones in the British Isles are now rare, but there are three magnificent examples (c1870–80) at Bristol (Plate 32)—a mixture of Indian, Gothic and Classic styles, justifiably earning them the Victorian title of 'Temples of Convenience'. There used to be an equally elaborate one at Dumfries in Scotland, dating from the 1880s or 1890s, but it was taken down in 1934.

More usual than the round (Plate 33) are the oblong ones, although these are rapidly disappearing. There are some in Birmingham, Reading and Great Ayton in North Yorkshire, and Scotland still has a number. There is a fine one at Walkerburn in Peebleshire (now Borders), decorated with a Tudor strap-work

Plate 34 Typical of the now fast-disappearing, cast-iron men-only, this free-standing cast-iron urinal is decorated with an elaborate pierced strap-work design. Walkerburn, Borders, Scotland (*Royal Commission on the Ancient and Historical Monuments of Scotland*)

pattern made by the Saracen Foundry, Macfarlane's Patent, Glasgow; and a rather plainer one with its top panels decorated in a pierced design put up by George Smith & Co, Sun Foundry, again of Glasgow (Plate 34). This firm was also responsible for an ornate example at Harbour Place at Burntisland in Fife, which is carried out in the usual mixture of styles. The front walls are embossed with Renaissance motifs, pierced with sunflowers (the symbol of the 1880s Arts and Crafts Movement) and topped by a Gothic rail. Unfortunately one panel is broken and the whole thing uncared for. These, and others like them in Scotland, are listed by the Royal Commission on the Ancient and Historical Monuments of Scotland; it is an encouraging sign that even such a humble artefact as a Victorian urinal should now be considered an Ancient or an Historical monument.

Another body conscious of old street furniture is the Camden Historical Society, which lists many pieces in London, one being a decorated cast-iron lavatory in Star Yard off Chancery Lane.

Among others still in London, but probably under sentence of destruction, is the one on Chelsea Embankment at the western end of Cheyne Walk, and another near Park Lane. Of the many that have gone, a fine one stood at Petty France and another outside Smithfield Meat Market. The latter stood on an 'island' with a horse trough, surrounded by bollards, but now only the bollards remain.

In recent years, in men's lavatories, there has been a move away from the old china or marble 'stalls' in favour of individual china or steel basins. These are, in fact, only a revival of the cast-iron basins that were a feature of the 1880s and 1890s, few of which remain. Here it is worth noting that even at that time, when sewerage was much improved, McDowell Steven & Co, Architectural Iron Founders and Sanitary Engineers (Contractors to Her Majesty's War, Prisons and Indian Departments) at Milton Iron Works in Glasgow (established in 1834), in its 1886 catalogue was offering a Dry Pan Closet Range 'particularly adapted for Towns, etc, where a regular water supply cannot be had, and where the absence of sewers would render our Water Closet System unsuitable'.

As well as these small iron, wooden or tiled lavatories, there were, and still are, many more larger and more solid structures with provision for 'Ladies' and 'Gentlemen'. Among them are such curiosities as those resembling Tudor cottages or battlemented castles; a nice little 'Ladies' in Kensington High Street in the latter style was pulled down as recently as 1977.

Jennings was also responsible, as our opening paragraph noted, for the first ever underground lavatory (for both sexes). By the 1890s underground lavatories for men and women were general, and they are still to be found all over the country, either at the side of the road or on 'islands'. Those in Holborn ('Gentlemen' on an 'island', 'Ladies' on the roadside) in London were put up in 1897. The entrances are surrounded by typically ornate iron railings with archways, which once carried globe lights with the appropriate sexes painted on the glass. Although listed, they are slowly decaying, the archway of the 'Ladies' being badly bent. Here one can see what look like lamp-posts without lamps, but they are in fact ventilation shafts. As an exception to this tall variety, there is a low Gothic-style dome-shaped one between a pair of lavatories at Holborn Viaduct. These, although freshly painted, are for some reason kept locked.

Perhaps the grandest ones in London used to be in Piccadilly Circus. Although underground, their upper parts were marvels of Victorian bombast, consisting of iron domes, five-globed lamps on pillars, and all manner of what were called 'enrichments' in the form of griffins, mouldings, friezes and festoons. These disappeared when the circus was remodelled between 1907 and 1927.

Several of these underground conveniences have suffered ignominious fates. Those on the Parade near the Abbey in Bath are now barely recognisable as such; their stone surrounds, with eighteenth-century-style balustrades, are still there, but their entrances are filled in, so that all remains are two sets of useless masonry—except that people can sit on them. A particularly elaborate stone surface 'Gentlemens' opposite the Theatre Royal in the same city has, recently been closed, owing to vandalism or because of goings-on, or both.

Many of these underground lavatories are in a dilapidated state, a particular disgrace being the pair of Gothic-style 'Men' and 'Women' in the Market Place in Cambridge. Oddly, though, however unkempt the ironwork may be, the attendant usually keeps the brass stair rail shining bright. Although not part of the street, the internal fittings of most underground lavatories used to be glories of marble, brass and glass, but most of these have been replaced by modern antiseptic alternatives. An exception is the already mentioned 'Gentlemen's in Holborn, which still retains its grey marble closets and 'stalls', the glass cisterns above the latter being supported on ever-bright brass columns. These stalls are interestingly marked 'George Jennings' Patentee', so that his name is perpetuated in at least one of his great benefits to mankind, although his Sanitary Engineering Company has now gone out of business.

The lavatories on the west side of Kensington Gardens in London are not only fitted with a lamp over the entrance but the tiles in the entry are printed with, of all things, eight bars of Beethoven's Ninth Symphony, a setting to music of Schiller's *An die Freude* or *Ode to Joy*. However inexplicable, it is a nice imaginative touch, rarely to be found today, although the much-modernised 'Gents' at Leicester Square displays a mosaic portrait of William Hogarth, who used to live in the square. An unusual pair of lavatories is to be found at the end of West End Lane in London NW8. Instead of the usual rather high railings, they are surrounded by brick walls and low railings that support wire-meshed domes, making them look for all the world like cages in a zoo. An example of 'half' preservation is the fact that one of the iron-railinged underground lavatories on the pavement at Turnham Green in London has been filled in and planted with flowers and plants like a miniature park.

Ironic footnote. In October 1977 a £25 reward was offered by Stafford's Town Council for the capture of the vandals who had wrecked their so called 'vandal-proof' public lavatories!

4. All lit up

In 1975, when Covent Garden Market in London was abandoned and the fate of most of its buildings was in question, the following poster was displayed on hoardings around the site:

> Westminster Council want to get *rid* of the *gas lights* in Covent Garden. If you like *gas lights* make the effort to write to Westminster and tell them so!

In fact, far from wanting to get rid of them, the Highways and Works Committee of the City Council had already, in September 1974, agreed to take no further action in respect of the lamps in the Covent Garden area for 2 years. Whether or not the appeal was effective, the North Thames Gas Board (which is the City Council's maintenance contractor) stated in 1975 that it would continue to maintain the gas units—even to the extent of installing replicas if the old ones, comprising over forty lights, wore out—for an indefinite period.

This concern over preserving old lighting fixtures by both public and official bodies is of comparatively recent origin. As far as the remaining examples are concerned, it is a question of, as Queen Victoria said on another occasion, 'Too little, too late'. In the early days of gas street lighting its promoters had to contend with great opposition, springing mainly from innate conservatism and prejudice, and the reluctance of councils to spend public money on what they considered an extravagance.

As an extreme example of prejudice, the following extraordinary document was published in Cologne in 1816, 14 years after the first English gas lights had lit up the street outside the engineering works of Boulton & Watt in Birmingham. Called *Arguments against Light* the text of this pamphlet evokes the voice of the seventeenth-century Catholic Church denouncing Galileo. Although obviously happy with such 'artificial' aids to light as fire, candles and oil, the author maintained that 'artificial illumination was an attempt to interfere with the divine plan of the world, which had pre-ordained darkness during the night-time'. Under what he called 'Judicial' (for which read 'Financial') objections he considered that people who did not want such light ought not to be compelled to pay for it. On 'Health' grounds he asserted that street lighting, by encouraging more people out of doors, would displace the natural fear of darkness so that 'drunkenness and depravity' would increase. (He ignored the fact that darkness had generally been held to encourage these activities.) He finished with the assumption that from the view of the common people 'the constant illumination of streets by night would rob festive occasions of their charm'.

In the ancient world street lighting in the form of oil lamps was used only during festivals and on religious occasions. For centuries such street lighting as there was tended to be mobile, carried in the form of torches or lanterns (lanthorns) by individuals, night-watchmen, or by men or boys employed by those who could afford them. In 1405 an attempt was made in England to have lanthorns hung on poles outside houses; the Court of Common Council decreed that they be hung out for the Christmas Watch and on saints' days—so that they were, as in Roman times, more a way of registering a religious festival than helping people in the dark. In 1415 a more stringent measure ordered those households whose property was rated at over £10 a year to burn candles outside their homes.

In the sixteenth century beacons or fire-buckets, called cressets, were much in use. One of these is still mounted on the tower of the church at Monken Hadley in Greater London. It is said to have been put up in 1588 to warn the locals of the approach of the Spanish Armada, and was lighted to celebrate the present Queen's coronation in 1953. These cressets were also hung on poles or carried by watchmen (such as Shakespeare's Dogberry in *Much Ado About Nothing*), who often carried a halberd for protection. In 1599, in addition to lanthorns, householders whose houses faced the street were expected to keep a lighted candle in the window between 6 and 9 o'clock on winter nights.

Things had not improved by 1679, when a clearly exasperated lord mayor of London lamented the 'neglect of the inhabitants of this city in hanging and keeping out their lights'. This neglect, he poetically asserted, allowed the 'sons of Belial' to 'wander forth . . . flown with insolence and wine'.

A slight advance, however, had previously been made in the shape of a new convex lantern (earlier ones had been flat-paned), perfected by one Edward Hemming, who was granted a licence in 1674 to erect one between every tenth house, to work from 6pm to midnight from Michaelmas Day (September 29) to Lady Day (March 25). But a vested interest in the form of the Tallow Chandlers Company was soon up in arms. It petitioned the lord mayor and aldermen of the City of London and, for good measure, the House of Commons itself, objecting to the fact that 'lucindaries' like those of Mr Hemming were 'merely novel' and would harm not only the Chandlers but such other trades as the Horners and Tinmen, who made the older lanthorns. The Chandlers said that lanthorns were cheaper than any other sort of lamp. They quoted Magna Carta. They pointed out the destructiveness of monopolies—conveniently ignoring the fact that they were trying to preserve their own. But officialdom was not wholly sympathetic to the 'plight' of the Tallow Chandlers, or for that matter to that of the Horners and Tinmen, and in 1686 they allowed the Admiralty to put up a convex light (which is still there) over the main gate of Deptford Dockyard.

Eventually, however, the opposition succeeded and Hemmings' licence was revoked in 1716. The London authorities had then to think up an alternative (not the only time that public bodies have been shamed into action by private enterprise), while not antagonising the Tallow Chandlers of this world. They revived the order that householders with houses rated at £10 and those in charge of public buildings, on pain of a 5s (25p) fine, be responsible for installing lights—but again the response was poor. In 1711 Birmingham Council, more go-ahead, authorised the putting up of about 700 lights.

Plate 35 These giant wrought-iron snuffers or extinguishers, with hoops in which to balance lights, were used by link-men and are one of the most elegant pieces of street furniture bequeathed to us by the eighteenth century. Berkeley Square, London W1 (*Mansell Collection*)

Plate 36 A beautiful wrought-iron gateway with light-holder and snuffer; on the left is a rare sedan-chair lift. Outside Alfred House, Alfred Street, Bath, Avon (*Geoffrey N. Wright*)

It was not until some 30 years later that the lord mayor of London and the Common Council, concerned by the increase in nightly crime, petitioned Parliament to erect more lights. This resulted in an Act giving the City permission to install lamps that were to burn from sunset to sunrise. Beginning with fifty in 1750, the number soon rose to 15,000. (Later, for some obscure reason, the responsibility passed to the Commissioners for Sewers.)

Despite all this, for those who could afford it the main method of being lighted home was to be accompanied by a link-boy or man who carried a flaming torch dipped in pitch, which he extinguished on arrival at the outsize snuffers that stood at the gateways or doors of houses. Many of these elegant examples of street furniture are luckily still to be found all over the country, where eighteenth-century houses have been allowed to retain them (although some have been altered or converted into electric lamps). There are some lovely ones in Berkeley Square in London (Plate 35), in Bath (Plate 36), and in other spas and old towns. This practice of link-lighting may have been safe in theory but in practice it had its built-in danger. As the poet John Gay put it:

> Though thou are tempted by the linkman's call
> Yet trust him not along the lonely wall,
> In the midway he'll quench his flaming brand,
> And share the booty with the pilf'ring band.

Lighting was particularly needful at the many turnpike and toll gates that punctuated so much of the road system of the eighteenth and early nineteenth centuries. Many of the old lamps and standards still to be found on our roadsides may well be relics of this era, even if, by now, they have been converted to electricity.

Gas Lighting

As already mentioned, the first example of exterior gas lighting in England was on the premises of the Birmingham engineering firm of Boulton & Watt. As part of the general festivities held to mark the Treaty of Amiens in 1802, William Murdock, a company employee who had taken out a patent for producing gas light from coal in 1791—lighting which had been used successfully inside the works—arranged for the outside to be lit by gas in a 'variety of ornamental devices'. This lighting immediately became the centre of attraction for vast crowds, many of whom came from outlying districts, the illumination providing, as one contemporary writer expressed it, 'a grand luxurious spectacle which astonished by its brilliance'.

Although in 1808 Murdock was given the Royal Society gold medal for his services to science in respect of his work with gas lighting, it was someone else who was to put it into general practice. This was Frederick Albrecht Winzer, a German who had come to

England in 1803. The first evidence that he had his eye fixed firmly on the main chance was the fact that he changed his name to the English form of Albert Winsor. His aim was to form a National Light and Heat Company by selling 20,000 £50 shares, amounting to the preposterously large sum of £1 million. Winsor used every kind of subterfuge and publicity trick. Although no technician or scientist, he claimed to have made great improvements in his patent light stoves by purifying the gas from all 'scent'—which was quite untrue, as the offensive smell of gas, even out of doors, was to be one of the many obstacles to its general acceptance. He gave lectures (read for him because his English was so poor) at which he distributed pamphlets. In prophetic words he urged that 'with the patronage of you and your friends, a national concern will soon be raised to open a mine of wealth in Britain'. On 26 June 1805 (which he had noted was George III's birthday) he succeeded in running a 1½in pipe from his house to the wall dividing it from the Prince Regent's Carlton House, which was later to become one of the first private buildings to have its façade lit by gas. Alas, both house and lights have gone.

But it was not until the end of 1807 that Winsor was granted permission to demonstrate this lighting publicly in fashionable Pall Mall, where he put up thirteen elegant hollow iron lamp-posts, each fitted with three globes. Although these have vanished (unless someone, somewhere, unwittingly has one), we know what they

Plate 37 In 1807 Albert Winsor erected London's first gas lamps in Pall Mall. This event was lampooned in 1809 by Rowlandson and Woodward in this famous cartoon. The spectators, in the main, are expressing objections—from the man who claims that the Thames will be 'burnt down', to the prostitute who declares that she might as well 'shut up shop' (*Mansell Collection*)

looked like from the cartoon by Rowlandson and Woodward (Plate 37). The *Monthly Magazine* reported the 'opening': 'The light produced by these gas lamps was clear, bright and colourless, and from the success of this experiment it may be entertained that this long-talked of mode of lighting may at length be realised.' Crowds blocked Pall Mall until nearly 12 o'clock, 'much amazed and delighted'.

Nowadays, off Pall Mall in Crown Court and Mall Passage, one can still see bracket lamps, which, if not as old as 1807, are at least among the earliest of exterior gas lamps still with us. Their preservation is a matter of concern.

After the spectacular and popular opening people began to buy shares, from the aristocracy to the very Tallow Chandlers themselves. Lady Bessborough bought five shares, summing it all up with the fine phrase: 'That shining lamp which has lit up Pall Mall for this year past has all at once blaz'd up into a comet that bears everything along with it.'

This 'comet' bore Winsor to the height of being at last allowed to form his company, although his application to Parliament for a charter in 1809 was rejected. One of the objectors was, not surprisingly, Murdock himself, understandably jealous and perhaps piqued that a foreign upstart had taken his own invention so far. Nothing daunted at the rejection, Winsor floated his own company in 1810, and by 1812 saw it officially recognised as the Gas, Light and Coke Company. Its first 'works' were at Cannon Row in Westminster, and its next at Peter Street, which premises were almost demolished by a gas explosion. The disaster was investigated by a committee of the Royal Society, one of whose members went so far as to say that the explosion proved that 'coal-gas could never be safely applied to the purpose of street lighting'. Despite this and other damning witnesses, Winsor was not drummed out of court and the committee made the sensible recommendation that if gas lighting were to become prevelant, then the reservoirs (now called gasometers) be small, numerous and separated from each other by party walls.

There was now no stopping gas street lighting. Most of the criticism, ill-founded fears, jokes, cartoons and ridicule petered out. In 1813 Westminster Bridge was lit by gas and in the following year Westminster Parish set the example for the general use of gas lighting by substituting gas for oil in its street lamps. Ten years later there were more than 30,000 gas lights in London alone, causing William Matthew in his *Compendium of Gas-Lighting* of 1827 to state that 'the advantages of . . . lights are particularly obvious in their resplendent effect in the public street'.

Many of these early gas lamps are still to be found in sheltered courts, alleyways and lanes up and down the country. Those in New College Lane in Oxford are good examples of old lamps having survived in a city because they are off the beaten track. These have Classic square lanterns topped by finials and supported by curved arms. But most are in a sad state of disrepair, unpainted, and rusty, their 'windows' either broken or hanging loose. At one bend in the lane there is the unusual juxtaposition of a lamp-post and similarly shaped wall-bracket side by side. Some of these lamps were made in the 1870s by the firm of Dean & Son (which also made drain covers), a small foundry situated in Temple Street in Oxford. It originated in Woodstock, where it made agricultural implements, but with growing industrialisation the firm moved into Oxford in the 1860s and changed over to making only street furniture. Other lamps of the same design were made by the Lucy Eagle Ironworks, which began business in 1825. Their lamps carry either this name or its earlier one, 'The Iron and Brass Foundry'. Up to 1889 the bases carried two shields: that for the City, embellished with an ox and a river; that for the University, comprising three crowns and a book. After this date, when the Oxford Corporation became the sole elected authority, the bases carried only the city shield and the words 'Oxford Corporation'.

Other cities, towns and boroughs were proud to have their own distinctive styles in lamp-posts. St James's Park in London has fifty-three gas lamps, many of them elegant George IV examples, which were put up in 1822. Those still in nearby Carlton House Terrace were erected to celebrate the accession of William IV in 1830, and, like the bollards of the same period (Plate 76), have distinctive bases carrying 'IV WR'. The City of London lamps display a griffin, Westminster lamps have a lacy frill around the top (although this style is fairly common throughout the country), Islington's and Paddington's lamps have piecrust edges, the Royal Borough of Kensington's lamps sport appropriate crowns, while those in Southwark have a fluted post and a wide bar below the lamp, and only one half if the post is set against a wall. Birmingham, whose famous Bull Ring has been so drastically rebuilt that many old buildings and street furniture have been swept away, used to have lamps with domes, pinnacles and crowns, and Newcastle lamps were also crowned.

Many lamp-posts throughout the country are entwined with dolphins: there are examples at Taunton, on Cambridge's immensely tall first electric lamp-post (put up in 1906) in Parker's Piece, and on lamps on St George's Plateau in front of St George's Hall in Liverpool. These last were originally made in 1851 and needed as many as eight sections. They were eventually converted to electricity in the early 1970s, but were in such bad repair that in 1972 the Lighting Department of the City made new ones from the original moulds. Alas, they omitted the orbs and crosses, as well as substituting blackish perspex globes for the former glass. Even so, fifty-eight of them form an elegant piece of planning, a touch of restrained flamboyance offsetting the severity of the 1839 Neo-classic building. In addition to Oxford's already mentioned neglected lamps of the 1870s and 1880s, this city can boast some unusual Art Nouveau (c1890) examples in many of its main thoroughfares. They are tall simple structures, the lamps hung from a long iron arm, and are shaped in a back curve so redolent of the style. Those posts ranged down the centre of St Giles have two such arms, but here, as elsewhere, many of the lamps themselves are modern.

It is surprising how few examples of old lamps (or indeed street furniture of any kind) are to be found in some of our oldest

Plate 38 One of the fine 'Gothic' 1862 lamps on Lendal Bridge in York; it closely resembles those on Westminster Bridge in London (*Kershaw Studios*)

'historic' cities, towns and villages. York is an exception, but Canterbury is woefully lacking in any sort of lamp, except for some pretty twirly ones tucked away in a park. Brighton, too, is thin on the ground as far as old lamps are concerned, although those in the grounds of the Pavilion have something of that building's eccentric charm, and the ones on the promenade have the appropriate look of spiky sea-urchins.

Old gas and electric lights have been spared on many bridges. Apart from those on the most recent version of London Bridge, the majority of the capital's bridges carry their original lamps. Those on Westminster Bridge are suitably 'Gothic', complementing the nearby 1840s 'Gothic' Houses of Parliament. There are galleon-decorated ones on Lambeth Bridge, and single-globed, crown-topped examples on the bridge over the Serpentine in Hyde Park. York has some splendid specimens: those on Lendal Bridge, which was built in 1862 and leads to the Minster, are 'Gothic' (Plate 38); while those on the Ouse Bridge are executed in an indefinite style. In summer the lamps on both these bridges, as well as other lamp-posts in the city, are happily decorated with flowering plants. The flamboyant 'Renaissance' bridge at Taunton in Somerset carries equally florid electric lamps similar to those on the Parade. There are some simple elegant iron lamps on the English Bridge built in 1774 over the Severn at Shrewsbury, and a pair of equally re-strained ones on the oldest iron bridge in the country, which is at Ironbridge. Although the now pedestrian-only bridge connecting Windsor with Eton has been given modern lamps, those on Barnes Pool Bridge in Eton High Street still carry four short 'Gothic' ones. Of these, two are without their lanterns and those which are complete do not work, light being provided by modern overhead or side lamps.

In the heyday of gas lighting, lamplighters in their hundreds were a familiar sight all over the country (Plate 47). Like such other public servants as postmen, dustmen, newspaper delivery boys and milkmen, they expected their Christmas 'box'. An 1830 broadsheet (probably written by a lighter himself) extolled the virtues and detailed the hardships of lamplighters, and urged people to be generous with their tips. The anonymous writer pointed out:

> To light in this enlightened age,
> Appears to me the rage.

He quite rightly assumed that most people took such men for granted:

> Whene'er you trip along the road so blithe and gay
> Returning home illum'd from hall or play
> Little do you think that ardourous toil and pain
> Is suffer'd by the lamplighter, this luxury to gain.

The lighter's lot was hard. He had to venture out in all weathers and often suffered accidents, but despite all this:

Forgetting what is past, he only hopes to know,
At Christmas he has many friends without a foe.

In the 1840s there was even a 'Lamplighter Schottische', the lithographed cover of the music sheet showing a man perched precariously on his ladder.

In 1977 there were still about 1,000 gas lamps in London. Westminster Parish has the most—400 around the Abbey, Smith Square and St James's Park. When the proposal was made that those around St James's Palace be converted to electricity for security purposes, it was turned down; instead, the Gas Board was

Plate 39 A granite-based lamp with a sexagonal lantern —with four 'arms' instead of the more usual two. Falmouth, Cornwall (*Robert Enever*)

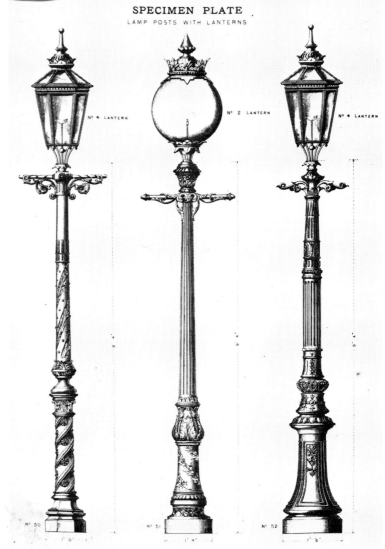

SPECIMEN PLATE
LAMP POSTS WITH LANTERNS

N° 4 LANTERN   N° 2 LANTERN   N° 4 LANTERN

N° 50   N° 51   N° 52

Plate 40 Renaissance-style lamp-post designs of the 1880s (*Mansell Collection*)

instructed to make them brighter! Six men look after all these lamps, resetting the automatic clock that switches the gas on and off. Only in the Temple, off Fleet Street (where some of the best early lamps in London are to be found), is there still a lamplighter carrying out his task in the old manual way. He is responsible for sixty-three lamps in the Inner Temple and forty in the Outer. When he began in the 1950s, there were over forty such lighters in London, but now the sole survivor, he is a tourist attraction in himself. It takes him about an hour to light these lamps, using a 7ft 100-year-old City of London torch, which is dipped in colza oil and methylated spirits.

After its slow gestation and difficult birth, street lighting at last produced a wealth of cast-iron, copper and tin lamps, brackets and

Plate 41 A sturdy and comparatively simple three-branched lamp-post which used to stand in Camden Town in London. Note the 'cannon' bollards. C1870 (*London Borough of Lambeth, Archives Department*)

Plate 42 The range of lantern designs in the 1880s was—apparently—limitless (*Mary Evans Picture Library*)

Plate 43 Lucky to survive because it is in a small town, is this self-confident—if stylistically far from 'pure' — two-branched lamp-post. Appleby, Cumbria (*Barbara Denness*)

Plate 44 One of a pair of elegant Art Nouveau lamp-posts outside a block of flats in West End Lane, London NW6 (*Author*)

posts that stagger at their zenith and surprise even now when the golden age is over and only relatively few examples remain. From the early pattern books—in 1823, along with the usual designs for railings and balconies, the *Smith and Founders Directory* was including Classically styled lamps—through engravings and drawings and up to photographs we can judge the range and sheer volume of styles and designs (Plates 39–44). The success of both gas and electric street lighting coincided with the greater use of cast iron, making virtually no design impossible—although some are 'impossible' indeed!

A visitor to London's outdoor tourist spots might be excused for thinking that street furniture, especially in the form of lamps, has by no means vanished. Trafalgar Square can claim the capital's most grandiose of lamps (Plate 45), and there are almost equally elaborate ones at the bottom of the Charing Cross Road and in Fleet Street. The Lower Regent Street and Admiralty Arch lamps sport appropriate galleons (Plate 46) while Art Nouveau lamps still light Long Acre and the Strand. These, being in St Martin's parish, carry a heavily moulded representation of the saint giving his cloak to a beggar. As with many lamps in other districts, some of these have the original posts but modern lanterns.

Perhaps the most famous of London lamps are those on the

Plate 45 A superbly flamboyant Renaissance-style candelabrum of a lamp-post which reminds us of the rich decorative work which was once general all over the country, though there were few as fine and as large as this. Trafalgar Square, London WC2 (*Author*)

Plate 46 As this post stands in front of Admiralty Arch in London, its pear-shaped globes are, appropriately, topped by a galleon (*Author*)

Plate 47 A once ubiquitious lamplighter tending one of the parapet lamp-posts put up in 1870 on the Victoria Embankment in London, and still there (*Mary Evans Picture Library*)

Plate 48 Some of the lamps which are modern copies of those on the opposite Victoria Embankment in London. King's Reach, Southwark SE1 (*Author*)

Victoria Embankment (Plate 47). Stretching between Westminster and Blackfriars Bridges, this embankment was designed by Sir Joseph Bazalgetter, chief engineer to the Metropolitan Board of Works, and built between 1864 and 1870 at a cost of £1,200,000. Not only did it appreciably narrow the Thames at this point, but it added another important thoroughfare to London, one of the few planned as a coherent whole. It was equipped with a series of exotic, dolphin-entwined three-globed lamps surmounted by crowns that are, alas, gone! The posts mounted on the parapet carry alternately the date 1870 and 'Vic Reg'. Some are now connected by loops of lights, which make this stretch of the river resemble a seaside esplanade. Unfortunately, even in 1900, these gas lamps were aided and abetted by some rather miserable little electric ones, but the flamboyance appropriate to a capital city still gives us a good idea of how so much of the rest of London (and other big cities) once looked. Similar, but much taller and less ornate, lamps stand along the embankment road. They are also decorated with Art Nouveau leaf designs and were made by Carron & Company (the early nineteenth-century cannon makers, see p 124).

As an indication of modern acceptance of the worth of these parapet lamps, when King's Reach on the South Bank of the river was overhauled in 1975, ten replicas (with crowns) were put up by the GLC. Incidentally, one of the original lamps is to be found in a far-away and unlikely spot; so taken by them was Sir Henry Isaac Butterfield, owner of Cliffe Castle in Yorkshire, that some time after their erection in London he managed to 'acquire' one for the entrance to his estate, where it still stands, and, although lacking its globe and crown, remains a strange echo of London opulence (Plate 48).

There are some extraordinary lamps on the Chelsea Embankment, where two figures appear to be climbing the post. Others there are Renaissance-style lamps that much resemble the three-globed ones standing in the courtyard of the British Museum. These are a sad reminder that similar lamps once lit the street outside.

Electric Lighting

Whereas it is possible to pinpoint almost exactly the first appearance of gas street lighting, it is surprisingly difficult where electricity is concerned. Short of contacting every city, town and borough in the country, it is impossible to discover where and when the first electric street lamp was installed, although many places make the claim.

Credit for the first electric light must go to Sir Humphry Davy, who in 1809 publicly demonstrated a 'most brilliant flame' from half an inch to $1\frac{1}{4}$in long from a Volva pile of 10,000 plates, although the experiment lasted for only a few minutes. It was not until some time between 1814 and 1844, however, that the new light was used to illuminate the streets of Paris. In England, in 1848, W. E. Staite gave demonstrations in Sunderland, and in the following year suspended an arc lamp from the north tower of Hungerford Bridge in London for 3 hours an evening for a fortnight; in the same year he did the same for Liverpool.

The first real success came in America in 1877, when a Mr Bush lit Cleveland's public square with arc lights. When Edison invented his lamp, the way was open and largely unchecked. In 1879 $1\frac{1}{4}$ miles of London, from Westminster to Waterloo, were lit by forty electric lights (many still there); and when Aldersgate Street Station was lit by electricity the crowd was so great that the police had to be called in. Single globe lamps were in use in Newcastle in 1881, the same year as the Siemens Brothers' experiment in London, when they were given the London Exchange area in which to erect six lights of 4,000 candlepower. The lamps were an astonishing 80ft high, each equipped with its own dynamo; though successful, they are no longer there. Between 1881 and 1882 Paddington, Charing Cross and Liverpool Street Stations were lit by electricity, as were parts of Liverpool, Bristol and Brighton. Even though the Government was largely opposed to electric street lighting, many companies were formed and 1882 saw the first Electric Lighting Act. In the same year Chesterfield claimed to be the only town in England to be wholly lit by electricity; it had 'Land-Fox' incandescent lighting in the churchyard and an arc lamp at St Mary's gate.

The story of how electric street lighting came to Taunton, in Somerset, is typical of many others, and points up the fact that private enterprise was responsible for a great deal of street furniture in the nineteenth century. Taunton's benefactor was H. G. Massingham, who owned shops there as well as in Bath. In 1885 he offered to light the Parade in Taunton for 1 month with the Thompson–Houston system of arc lighting, and these lamps were ordered from Laing, Wharton & Down of Holborn Viaduct in London, whose gratified representative pointed out that 100 companies in America and many on the Continent were already using this system but he had, up to then, received no orders from England, despite the fact that the system was automatic and little wear was incurred. The two-globed lamp standards were carried out in full-blown Renaissance-style, their bases entwined with dolphins. When first switched on in December 1885, the lights 'burned exceedingly steadily' from 5 o'clock until 11 o'clock in the evening.

Mr Massingham's example was soon followed by tradesmen in other parts of the town, who obviously saw the advantage of this kind of publicity. Although a Taunton Electric Lighting Company was formed in January 1886, Massingham went his own private-enterprise way, and in the spring of that year obtained permission to supply limited electric lighting at his own expense on the Parade. In December he entered into a formal contract with the corporation (which had obviously waited with caution to see if the whole venture were worth while) to light the streets of the whole town.

One of the greatest losses in lamps has been the bracket variety. These used to hang outside most public houses, shops, hotels and restaurants. Sometimes the often very ornate brackets remain but their lights have disappeared or been replaced by modern versions or signs. There are few left to compare with the splendid confident vulgar cheerfulness of the originals, with their engraved or painted globes or glass panels.

Some of the grandest, those on the front of the now gone 'Old King's Head' gin palace in Hampstead Road, London, were

Plate 49 One of the few lamps on an ornate bracket which used to be such a feature of shop fronts, hotels and restaurants. Even the pair of this one is lacking its central 'star'. Brady's Red Lion Hotel—now a public house, Kilburn High Road, London NW6 (*Author*)

Plate 50 Two typical shop-window lamps—very few of which are left (*Mary Evans Picture Library*)

Plate 50 Two typical shop-window lamps—very few of which are left (*Mary Evans Picture Library*)

D. HULETT & CO., LIM.

WHOLESALE AND EXPORT GAS FITTING MANUFACTURERS,

55 & 56 HIGH HOLBORN, LONDON.

HOSIER?

SHOP REFLECTING LAMP

DRAPER

SHOP WINDOW LAMPS.

Plate 51 Many private houses and entrances to parks or avenues still carry lamps fixed to arches. This lovely example of wrought-iron-maker's craft is, however, sadly damaged; retaining only one of its 'flowers' while the 'Gothic' lantern no longer works. Castle Street, Carlisle, Cumbria (*Barbara Denness*)

removed as early as 1906. One of the few public houses in London to retain such lamps is the 'Red Lion' in Kilburn High Road (Plate 49), which date from the building's reconstruction in 1890. Many, as these do, not only lit the fronts of the buildings but also advertised them. Such functions were also performed by the lamps that used to stand outside the Café Royal in Regent Street, and the many that graced practically every shop and store all over the country. There were some particularly fine ones in the High Street in Wandsworth, London, but they vanished, with practically everything else of interest, when the vast new Arndale Centre was put up in the 1960s.

Among lamp-posts and brackets everyone will have his or her own favourite pockets of resistance. Eton schoolboys can boast a beauty, the 'Burning Bush', which was put up in the middle of the road outside School Hall in 1864. It is a strange lamp, looking more like a market cross than anything else and, like such crosses, standing on three wide steps and a stone column. (It might well be on the site of fairs or markets that used to be held when Eton was founded by Henry VI in 1442.) Above the column is an elaborate wrought-iron structure—four barley-sugar columns topped by crowns, sprouting leaves and flowers—and in the centre is the lamp itself, giving the whole its nickname. In the 1950s, owing to

Plate 52 One of the elegant lamps which lights and decorates the north side of Drury Lane Theatre in London. The brackets cleverly echo the curves of the Ionic capitals on the columns which are said to have come from Nash's Regent Street, the colonnade which was shamefully demolished in 1848 (*Author*)

increased traffic, this rare lamp was moved to an 'island' and thence to a widened stretch of pavement, where it is now a mid-morning meeting place for boys awaiting masters.

Other old lamps are still protected because they are part of railings or buildings. In London, for instance, there are some fine ones around Hyde Park and on the Hyde Park Hotel, extremely elegant ones lighting the Royal Arcade off Pall Mall, and good ones hanging between the arches on Bedford Chambers in Covent Garden (Plate 50). Superb ones (some missing) are strung along the Ionic columns (said to have come from Nash's old Regent Street) that grace the north side of Drury Lane Theatre (Plate 52). Surely safe also are the lamps that light the lovely Colonnade in Bath Street in that city, and those in another of England's famous watering places, Royal Tunbridge Wells in Kent. Although often broken, many lamps are still to be found in the centre of iron arches spanning gateways to parks or private houses (Plate 51).

Equally safe, as it is such a tourist attraction, must be the large lamp that hangs outside, and proclaims the name of 'The Cheshire Cheese' public house in Wine Office Court (an Excise Office up to 1665) off Fleet Street. Among the best known of bracket lamps are the 'Blue Lamps', symbols of the Police Force, which are either still fixed to their original buildings or to modern ones, where their flamboyance is in striking contrast to the severity of their new surroundings. In 1976 a survey carried out in London listed the remaining examples—so that there is a strong chance that they, at least, will be preserved.

5·From pillar to post

Pillar Boxes and the Postal Service

Perhaps I was not unique as a small boy when I fondly imagined that when one posted a letter in a pillar box, it immediately travelled underground to its destination. A somewhat similar assumption that a pillar box was a thing of mystery (and therefore not to be trusted) was in the minds of many people when the first pillar boxes were introduced into the British Isles in 1852.

Several claims have been made as to who first instituted such boxes in the British Isles. Charles Reeves, a Scottish riding surveyor, had already made the suggestion in 1834, but the credit must certainly go to Anthony Trollope, the novelist, who was a surveyor's clerk in the Post Office. His idea was to start in the Channel Islands with 'letter boxes in posts fixed at the road side'. He proposed that they be made of iron, free-standing on corners or fitted into walls. George Greswell, Surveyor of the Western District of England, agreed with him, and by 1852 the first roadside boxes were put up in St Helier in Jersey and others in St Peter Port, Guernsey. Unfortunately not even a sketch of this first British pillar box remains, but the *Jersey Times* of 26 November 1852 gave a description, which was to apply to most of the boxes that followed. The box was sexagonal, 4ft high and made of cast metal. As well as a vertical slot for letters, three sides bore the Royal Arms, the words 'Post Office' and a sliding cover for the removal of the contents. The same newspaper also stated that 'these pillar boxes when completed (and it is high time that they should be) will be a great benefit to those of the public who reside at some distance from the General Post Office'.

The carefully preserved pillar box in Union Street in St Peter Port in Guernsey may well be an original survivor. These first boxes were mounted on blocks of granite (a common enough material in these parts) but later ones were made entirely of cast iron. Very like it is the 'Early Mainland' style (Plate 53) of 1853–6.

Although for some time there was to be conservative opposition, as with so many inventions once the idea had been seen to work, people became accustomed to it and soon relied on it. Pillar boxes were therefore erected all over the British Isles; at first principally at railway stations. In 1855 in London a number of square-sided

Plate 53 One of the first pillar boxes still with us—the 'Early Mainland' 1853–6, at Barnes Cross, Holwell, Dorsetshire. Only one other is known, and this is on private land in Plymouth. After 1856 there are only three examples of this style (*Geoffrey N. Wright*)

93

cast-iron boxes were put up. All these have gone, but the *Illustrated London News*—that invaluable record of all things new—published an illustration and description of the one at the corner of Fleet Street and Farringdon Street. It was, as the reporter put it, 'much less ornamental than the Paris pillar', being 'a stove-like design, reminding one of the latest London conduits'. It was ornamented on top by an upturned acanthus leaf and a ball, and fitted with an elaborate 'contrivance' for taking out the letters (equipped with Messrs Chubb's locks, which were called 'patent detectors'). The town delivery took (or was supposed to take) about $1\frac{1}{2}$ hours, and that to the suburbs from $1\frac{1}{2}$ to 3 hours 'from the time of despatch, according to distance'.

Other such boxes ran along the line of the thoroughfare of Ludgate Hill, Fleet Street, the Strand and Piccadilly 'on the side of the footway in such a position as not to obstruct traffic of any kind'. In 1856 the horizontal instead of the vertical slot was adopted; times of collections were put on iron plates the next year, although this was not general until 1871. By the late 1850s the total number of post boxes in England was only 703, but by 1861 there were 2,473. Although the first one had been red, the most usual colour was dark green until 1874, when the now prevailing red became standard.

An adequate and working postal system had been a long time a-coming, England being particularly slow in adopting new ideas. There was some sort of postal service in the sixteenth century, and a contemporary map shows the route for the carrying of letters from London to the north. It was probably not very efficient, and for centuries after this the only method of sending letters was by people who happened to be travelling in the direction of the recipient, by more-or-less regular messengers who (for a fee) travelled from town to town, and by the bell-men or boys in towns or villages who carried letters from house to house.

Monarchs had their own personal postal services. In 1635 Charles I allowed his private arrangement to be made available to the general public, but it is strange that the English, forever aping anything French—particularly their clothes—did not follow them when they introduced posting boxes in the streets of Paris as early as 1635. In London in 1680 it was still the custom for people to pay bell-ringers—their jangling instruments telling people that the letter-man was on his way carrying a bag with a slot in it for letters—and messengers to take letters to and collect letters from the coach on what were called 'Post Nights'. The latter was at least some advance.

In 1681 William Dockwra was the first Englishman to make an attempt to organise a proper service in London. Unfortunately it was declared illegal a year later, because it infringed the Duke of York's monopoly! Dockwra had, however, made his point, for he was subsequently given the management of the (limited) Government service. In 1709 Charles Povey set up a system in London, Westminster and Southwark that was called 'Half-Penny Carriage'. As with previous schemes, it was in direct opposition to the Government, as his post cost half the official price. Povey organised a team of bell-ringing postmen, although even this was suppressed only 7 months later; but, as so often, once given the lead by a private person, the Government then continued the practice itself. During the eighteenth century in London, General-Post Letter Carriers walked the streets for one hour in the evening for the night mails from London. One penny was charged for this over and above the postage, the man himself getting only 14s (70p) a week. These ill-paid carriers continued to collect and deliver mail until about 1866, long after a 'proper' system was introduced; they were much favoured (and their eventual loss much lamented), especially by country people, who had grown accustomed to them and had learned to trust them.

Post could also be delivered to, and collected from, post offices, which were called Post Receiving Houses, and, according to the *Illustrated London News* of 1855, of 'a very imperfect kind'; they were 'denoted by a richly-emblazoned pane, in which the time-honoured British lion shone in full national emblazonry'. By 1814 the Government had issued an instruction that every such 'house' or 'office' was to be fitted with a letter box with the words 'Unpaid Letter Box' painted on it. As the *News* put it, 'here and there the tutelar animal's [lion's] mouth was the receptacle of letters'. A wooden box which was once fastened to the wall of Lea Marston post office in Birmingham, is now in private hands. The oldest of these 'mouths', a simple iron slot with the date 1809 boldly embossed on it, is now in Wakefield Museum. It used to be fixed to the wall of the local post office in Wood Street, and was saved from destruction when the building was demolished in 1964. Another such box (or probably part of it) made of stone, is in the Great Yarmouth Museum, safely installed there in 1968 after it had stood on the wall of a building in High Street, Gorleston, since about 1831. But these metal or stone slots were rare, the post office window usually being merely fitted with a slit made in one of the window panes; the clerks whose job it was to collect and hand over letters through this aperture were (understandably) known as 'Window Men'. There were also unattended apertures through which one could put in one's letter and a penny for payment. Most of these were closed at night, as in troubled times they proved perfect receptacles for bombs or other incendiaries, a practice unfortunately not unknown today. By 1829 late letters were accepted at post office windows without the usual extra fee.

The advent of the Industrial Revolution had much to do with the increase in the number of post offices and letter boxes. With so

Plate 54 Only seven of these 1856–7 Doric column pillar boxes remain. At this time the slot was vertical. Beside East Gate (there is another at West Gate) in Warwick, Warwickshire (*Rosemary Atherton*)

Plate 55 An hexagonal Penfold pillar box which was put up between 1866–79. At the corner of Denton Road and Middleton Avenue, Ilkley, North Yorkshire (*Cressida Pemberton-Pigott*)

many families moving into towns or factory areas, letter writing (among the literate, that is) greatly increased, and the former irregular and haphazard system could not cope with the sudden flow. Rowland Hill's 1840 Penny Post did much to make things easier. He also proposed the setting up of roadside boxes away from post offices.

Until people and the authorities began to be interested in preserving them, many were just thrown away, but now, of all pieces of street furniture, the pillar box is the best documented. This is due to what is now called 'The Pillar Box Treasure Hunt' of 1964, instituted by Jean Young Farrugia, an employee in the Records Department of the GPO. In 1969 she wrote the most comprehensive book on the subject, to which I am indebted for most of the information in this chapter. Early in 1964 Mrs Farrugia discovered that only twenty-eight pillar boxes were recorded but, by the time the Hunt was completed, this had risen to over 600—excluding the many boxes from the 1880s to 1901, or those of this century, apart from the surprising 217 that were put up in the short reign (1936) of Edward VIII.

The Hunt was started by asking the readers of the *Post Office Magazine* to report any pillar boxes in their areas, but it was not long before the press, radio and television were joining in, resulting in over 200 letters. These enabled Mrs Farrugia to list every known pillar box from the few early ones, through the 'Non-Standards' of the 1870s to the 'Anonymous' cylindrical ones—anonymous because many carry no maker's name (Plate 56).

In style most of the early ones display such Regency restraint and Classicism as the elegant Doric column or pillar (possibly the reason for its being called a 'pillar box'); only seven of these are recorded (Plate 55), dating between 1856 and 1857. Simple hexagonal ones were in use at the same time, and in 1856 a special fluted one with a dome and a crown on the top was made for Birmingham; examples of these are now to be found only in museums. About this time Scotland was provided with even plainer boxes, although one of 1856 had a rather grand crown on the top. Only once have British pillar boxes been decorated with the lavishness one expects of Victorian design. This was more popular on the Continent; indeed some French, German and Belgian boxes were very exotic. The English 'fancy' one was made for London and the larger cities in 1857–9, but only three of them survive in the Post Office collection. They are hexagonal and decorated with a generous sprinkling of embossed flowers and an egg-and-dart pattern around the base of the capital or domed top. An 'economy' version (no frills whatsoever) was made by Cochrane & Company (responsible for so many boxes) for country towns, but you would have to live in or go to Cork in Ireland to see the last remaining example of this style.

The first National Standard box, much on present-day lines but with a rather heavy crude top, was made between 1857 and 1859; most of the remaining examples of this style are to be found in Liverpool. Then there is what was called the 'Liverpool Special', designed by Mr Gay, a district surveyor. This was also made by Cochrane but without Post Office approval, although, once cast, it was not rejected outright. It is tall and rather elegant, and topped by a fine crown. Mrs Farrugia lists only three in Liverpool and one in the Post Office collection.

We now come to the many pillar boxes—of which there were four variations (mainly of proportion)—designed by J. W. Penfold. Called 'Hexagonal Penfolds', they were put up between 1866 and 1879 (Plate 56). They are characterised by a sort of acanthus leaf on the dome, with or without a finial. The first one cost £7 18s 3d (£7.91) and the majority are in London, but other examples are still to be found from Truro to Birkenhead, the one there being known erroneously as a 'Trollope' box.

Apart from some square boxes—there is a handsome double Edward VII one outside the British Museum—most of the boxes from 1879 onwards are round or oval. Double aperture ones cannot date before 1899, when this type was first tried out in London; it had become general all over the country by 1905.

Of all pieces of street furniture, the pillar box has changed least with the times; those put up for Elizabeth II's reign, beginning in 1952, look exactly the same as those put up for her great-great-grandmother, Queen Victoria, in the 1880s. Only the changing royal ciphers show the progression of the years, although those for George V, for some reason, omit the number.

Despite all these official boxes, there were several alternatives, such as the one in Cambridge 'decorated' with seventy-five spikes along its top. Rochdale boasts one with a lamp-post on it, and there is a large stone version standing on a grass 'island' in the centre of the village of Nether Winchendon in Buckinghamshire. Round and topped by a low pinnacle surmounted by an iron ball, its posting part is an iron wall-type box made by the Eagle Foundry of Birmingham between 1871 and 1881. Private persons have also elected to put up their own boxes or at least to give character to the ones already there. In 1876 the Rev W. K. W. Chafy bought the estate of Rous Lench Court in Hereford and Worcester; outside the gates he had two Tudor-style pitched roof coverings put over wall boxes; at first sight they look very like the kind of shelters put up over so many wells.

Wall Boxes

The first of these, which are all simple upright iron oblongs with a receiving slot in them, were put up in 1858 in existing walls as a continuance of the old post box and as a cheaper alternative to

Plate 56 A high-aperture, 'anonymous' cylindrical pillar box, made between 1887 and 1904—a style which persists today in various sizes. Kimberly Park, Falmouth, Cornwall (*Robert Enever*)

the free-standing pillar. The first ever is still in use at The Mall, Newport, on the Isle of Wight. This was followed by a great number of versions, the difference usually only a question of size and a different arrangement of lettering, time-plates, etc. Many of these boxes are to be found in towns and cities but the majority are in country districts (Plate 57), where one can also find them—inspired by the American custom—fitted to stone posts on grass verges. Between 1896 and 1949 small wall boxes with rounded tops were fitted to many lamp or other posts by a couple of metal bands.

Stamp-vending Machines

These are to be found either in the walls of post offices or fixed to the sides of pillar boxes. After a few unofficial ones were put up between 1884 and 1887, the Postmaster-General in 1889 finally gave permission to install Collins' Automatic Stamp Deliverer on some London pillar boxes but only if a proposed advertisement for Pears' Soap was not included! By the 1890s the machines became more general under the Stamp Distribution Syndicate Ltd (Plate 58).

As a nice example of (one hopes) undying British eccentricity, one George Corner spent much of his life leapfrogging over pillar boxes, and was still doing so at the age of 77 in 1977. To celebrate his 75th birthday, he jumped over a box in King Street in Hudders. field, West Yorkshire, dressed up as Robin Hood for the occasion- He claimed to have jumped over nearly 1,000 British pillar boxes in his time.

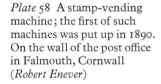

Plate 57 A wall letter box fastened to a brick post; others are found set into whole walls. Made between 1881 and 1904. Hexham, Northumberland (*Barbara Denness*)

Plate 58 A stamp-vending machine; the first of such machines was put up in 1890. On the wall of the post office in Falmouth, Cornwall (*Robert Enever*)

6· Timepieces

Sundials

People tend to associate sundials only with 'olde worlde' gardens. But as many, if not more, were put up in public places, not only before they were the only way of telling the time but also well into the twentieth century.

The earliest, often Saxon, ones are to be found on the walls of churches, where they were incised into the stone and given the usual central iron marker or 'gnomon', some of which are now missing. These dials were not only helpful for passers-by but were used by the bell-ringer so that he could call people 'to the church on time'. For this reason they are called 'mass dials', the longest incised line being about 9 o'clock, the usual time for the service. Most are rather crude, such as the pair at Long Wittenham in Oxfordshire, but there is a fine fourteenth-century example on the wall of a church at North Stoke near Goring in Oxfordshire,

Plate 59 A fine example of an old and new method of telling the time, side by side. On the fourteenth-century church at Weobley, Hereford and Worcester (*R. H. Pye*)

where the dial is supported by sculpted hands and topped by the sculpted head of a man. There is a very elaborate eighteenth-century one detailing the movements of the sun and moon etc, and surrounded by lovely rococo stone decorations, on the wall of the ruined church of All Saints at Isleworth in Greater London. Certainly in the 'olde worlde' category is the medieval-style dial that was put up on the wall of a church at St Wenn in Cornwall in 1855, when 'Gothick' was so fashionable. In 'olde' style it bears the message 'Ye know not when', and the date is written in Roman numerals.

Sundials are also to be found on the walls of inns: there is a metal one on the front of what is now a private house but was once the 'King's Head' at London End, Beaconsfield, in Buckinghamshire. Sundials were also added to stone columns, and a few of

Plate 60 This elevated sundial, complete with lion-supported seat, was put up in 1730 at Drakelowe Hall in Burton-on-Trent in Staffordshire but removed to York in 1953 (*Author*)

Plate 61 A fine 1682 market 'cross' topped by a sundial and a brightly painted lion. Note the turret clock in the background, dated 1800. Carlisle, Cumbria (*Barbara Denness*)

these remain: there is a fine early eighteenth-century example on a sixteenth-century bridge óver the River Wye at Wilton in Hereford and Worcester. It carries the kind of chilling reminder of mortality that is so much a feature of sundials:

> Esteem thy precious time which pass [sic] so swift away,
> Prepare thou for Eternity and do not make delay.

Known to have been put up in 1730 is the sundial on a pillar, with a seat at its base, which stands on College Green in York (Plate 60). It formerly stood at Drakelowe Hall at Burton-on-Trent in Staffordshire, but the Friends of York Minster gave it to the city in 1953. For some strange reason a sundial tops a Gothic-style monument standing near the Causeway at Kellaways in Wiltshire. It commemorates one Maud Heath, who, although only a pedlar woman born in nearby Langley Burrell, left enough when she died in 1474 to pay for the medieval stone causeway with sixty-four arches that still stands in the often-flooded area between Wick Hill and Chippenham.

Sundials also appear on the top of market crosses, especially those made in the seventeenth century, which are not really 'crosses' at all but columns with capitals of one of the three Classical orders. There is a sundial surmounted by a ball on top of a vaguely Doric column in Great Staughton in Cambridgeshire, which is dated 1631. The one at Ilchester in Somerset has a capital of no known order, but does date from the seventeenth century; it also carries a ball and weathervane. There is a Doric example at Boroughgate, Appleby, in Cumbria, and a splendid 1682 one at Carlisle in the same county. The latter (Plate 61) is very imposing, although its sundial, topped by a carved and painted lion, looks somewhat incongruous and top-heavy. Most of these elegant columns are so tall that it is difficult to imagine that their dials were ever of much use.

Not in the street, but worth noting, is the dial on a square stone pillar standing in Petts Wood in Greater London. This one is not likely to vanish (except through vandalism), as the wood in which it stands is under the protection of the National Trust. It is an appropriate memorial to William Willett, who is buried in Chislehurst churchyard, as it was he who advocated 'daylight saving', a measure adopted after his death in 1915.

Clocks

Many more street clocks than sundials are still with us, but they are now often purely decorative, as many of them no longer work or do so only intermittently. Even when clocks began to replace sundials, conservative people were slow to accept them (for one thing a clock was so much more expensive to install and maintain), so that one often finds the early sundial still in place next to a later clock (Plate 61). Very early clocks often have no hands at all, the time being given only by the striking hours and quarters—useless if one were nowhere near the clock when it sounded. Among this kind still in position is the one on the church in Cookham in Buckinghamshire, and another on the south tower of the church of St Leonard-at-the-Hythe in Essex, which was put up about 1500. The next step was a single handed clock of which only about twenty examples remain in this country. That on the church in Sutton Courtenay in Oxfordshire dates from about 1600, and was given a new dial and two hands as late as 1950. There is another on the church tower in Northill in Bedfordshire and the one on the church of the Holy Cross at Felsted in Essex bears the following inscription on its works: 'Johannes Fordham De Dunmow Magan Fecit Anno 1701'. Also in Essex is the one-handed eighteenth-century clock that carries the motto 'Sans Dieu Rien'. It is now on a wooden cupola on the Record Office at Ingatestone Hall. Another example of a clock having been moved is that on the tower of St Peter's Church in Wallingford in Oxfordshire; it was bought by a local landowner from no less a place than Horseguards Parade in London.

Minute hands were not in general use on public clocks until the eighteenth century, and even then they were often made of wood, which, being perishable, had to be renewed every 50 years or so. There are so many examples of 'perfect' clocks—practically every Town or Guild Hall or other public building in the country being equipped with one—that it would be tedious to enumerate them. A curiosity is the triangular wooden (probably eighteenth-century) clock on the church at Whitgift near Goole in Humberside, which shows in Roman numerals the hour of thirteen instead of twelve. Alas, some of our clocks have vanished through being sold to America. A clock made in 1828, which used to adorn the tower of St Mary's church in Hambledon, was sold to Detroit in 1948. The most famous (or infamous) example of selling our heritage was when the hanging clock at Victoria Station in London (not in the street) was sold to a San Francisco restaurant owner in 1971, thus robbing London of one of its best known and most popular meeting places.

Clocks on cupolas or in little towers often appear on town halls, large houses, stables and other such buildings. The one on the Town Hall at Amersham in Buckinghamshire carries a weathervane, as does that on the Moot (or assembly) Hall at Brampton in Cumbria, which was built in 1817. The one on the roof of a building in Abinger Hammer in Surrey also carries the figure of an iron man who strikes the bell with a hammer, the surrounding district having once been famous for iron forging. A similar figure can be found on the clock on a house on the Guildford–Dorking Road in Surrey where a blacksmith hits the bell. The clock carries the following message to tardy travellers: 'By me you know how fast to go'. An 1890s clock above a shop front in London's Old Kent Road is fixed into the middle of an iron man, and an electric mechanism makes him lift his hat at 1 o'clock every day. Such 'fancy' clocks are very likely to stay (and to work) as they are showpieces that 'natives' and tourists like to watch in operation as the hours are struck by various little figures. In London the most popular are those on the façade of Fortnum & Mason's in Piccadilly, on the 'Elizabethan' façade of Liberty's in Regent Street, in Cheapside and on the church of St Dunstan-in-the-West in Fleet Street. A grand looking sixteenth-century one-handed clock with

Plate 62 An elaborate clock decorated with particularly delicate ironwork. It was put on the medieval walls of Chester to celebrate Queen Victoria's 1897 Diamond Jubilee (*Barbara Denness*)

sun, moon and stars on its face (called 'Matthew the Miller') on the tower of St Mary Steps church in Exeter in Devon has its hours struck by figures set in niches. Then there is the 'Quarterboy' clock on the tower of the former St Martin's church (now an information bureau) at Carfax in Oxford, below which two little metal boys strike the quarters. A similar pair strike bells above the clock face on Wells Cathedral.

Returning to turret and cupola clocks, the one at Great Dunmow in Essex has a bell made by one Bryan Eldridge in 1651, and in the village of Great Holland in the same county, on a building that was once the local baths, is a clock which used to time each person's sixpennyworth of dip. At Coalbrookdale in Salop a fine turret clock with a gold ball on the top adorns a great warehouse erected in 1843. Inns were also favourite and obvious sites for such clocks; the Crown Inn at Marlow carries one that came from the original Market House. Many of the most elaborate are in full-flown Victorian Gothic. The gateway to the Bishop's Palace in Bishop Auckland, County Durham, has a clock turret with castellations and pinnacles. There is a magnificent iron affair on the famous medieval walls of Chester, which was presented to the city by Edward Evans-Lloyd, citizen and freeman, to mark Queen Victoria's 1897 Diamond Jubilee (Plate 62).

Clock Towers

This category includes only those towers that are complete in themselves and not part of a building, although one can't leave out the most famous clock tower in the world, part of the Houses of Parliament, London, containing the bell Big Ben as its shape and style influenced many a clock tower all over the country. Although considerably smaller, there are many such in Birmingham, and a veritable giant at Machynlleth in Powys was put up by the 5th Marquess of Londonderry to celebrate the coming of age of his eldest son, Viscount Castlereagh, in 1873—at a time when the aristocracy could afford to make such grandiose gestures. Such gestures were also made by borough councils or paid for out of public subscriptions to honour public figures.

Overlooking the harbour at Swanage in Dorset is a curious medieval-looking tower, which, in the November 1938 issue of the *Port of London Authority Monthly*, is referred to as 'a Gothic Bell Tower which used to stand on the south side of London Bridge'. Indeed it did, but the Port of London people should have done a bit more homework, for this 'bell tower' was originally the Wellington Testimonial clock, carried out in very elaborate Victorian Gothic, and erected in 1854 to commemorate the first Duke of Wellington, who had died two years previously. £1,500 was collected by public subscription to pay for it to be put up in the centre of the roadway opposite Duke Street and Southwark Cathedral. But by 1865 it was already considered to be a traffic hazard and, stripped of its clock, spire and ornamental saints, it was removed to its present position. The lack of the clock and the fact that the spire was replaced by an incongruous little dome must have led the magazine to make its mistake.

Queen Victoria's Jubilees of 1887 and 1897 gave an excuse for erecting many a clock tower. One of the grandest 1897 examples, now a landmark, must be the one in the centre of Brighton in East Sussex (Plate 63). Made of stone and granite it is embellished with mosaic portraits of the Queen, Prince Albert (dead for 36 years then) and Edward and Alexandra (Prince and Princess of Wales), while female statues symbolise Industry and Virtue. It is a truly

Plate 63 One of the most elaborate of clock-tower memorials erected for Queen Victoria's 1897 Jubilee. It is a mixture of classic, Romanesque and what-have-you styles with, for good measure, public lavatories at its base. North Street, Brighton, East Sussex (*Barbara Denness*)

magnificent example of Victorian self-confidence combined with utility, for in addition to its clock it has underground public lavatories at its base. Many clock towers in Victorian Gothic style look as if they have lost their churches. Such a one stands in the middle of the road at Grimston in Norfolk, where it was put up for the 1897 Jubilee. An oddity is the miniature Big Ben's style of clock that is balanced on a Corinthian column at Cricklade in Wiltshire. It was put up in 1897 and, for added interest, its pendulum swings in water. An unusual variation of this royal theme is the clock on the Saxon Tower of St Andrew's Minster, St Andrews, Scotland, which was put up in 1910 to mark the death of Edward VII.

A strange, perhaps Romanesque, tower with clock and drinking-fountain stands in splendid isolation in the middle of Tynemouth in Tyne and Wear. It was designed by Oliver and Lamb and erected in 1861, the year of the Prince Consort's death, although this fact is not mentioned (Plate 64). An 1842 tower with a broad base and a pyramid-shaped top stands at the bottom of the main street in Wendover in Buckinghamshire; and the tower at Rhayader in Powys is a strange amalgam of styles, its base a stone 'Grecian Temple' on which stands a brick column surmounted by an eighteenth-century cupola and a Gothic cross. The brick clock tower in the centre of Epsom High Street is in Romanesque style; a photograph of 1896 shows it in a rural setting, which has now been replaced by a very busy modern street. Very simple and severe is the slender brick battlemented tower that stands alone at

Plate 64 One of the many clock towers which appears to have lost its church. This one, in Romanesque style, also equipped with a drinking-fountain and horse trough, stands remotely in the centre of Tynemouth in Tyne and Wear (*Barbara Denness*)

Creetown in Dumfries and Galloway, the only modern note being a sign pointing to a nearby camping site. One of the oldest of belfry towers is the fifteenth-century one in St Albans in Hertfordshire, which was put up between 1403 and 1412 at what was once the centre of the medieval town.

One clock tower that has vanished quite recently is mentioned on p 116; it was put up in 1907 in St George's Circus, Southwark, London, to replace the eighteenth-century milestone obelisk. It was the gift of Messrs W. B. & R. Faulkner and many designs for it were submitted, each more a heavy muddle of styles than the last. Not that the winner was exactly a piece of pure architecture, its structure being 'Renaissance' and its dome Hindu Saracenic—a style then popular in British India. It was 70ft high, and made of Portland stone and Cornish grey granite; and its corners sported four electric 'Excello' arc lamps of 4,500 candlepower mounted on 'artistically' wrought iron brackets. It cost the Faulkner brothers £3,500, but when in 1937 it was considered a danger to traffic the borough council could not even give it away. It was therefore demolished and now nothing decorates the simple grass circle in the middle of busy St George's Circus.

A very early electric clock on top of a lamp-post-like column used to stand at the western end of the Strand in London, opposite the now preserved 'pepper-pot' Nash buildings. The clock was started on 1 September 1852, and became the pride of the Electric Telegraph Company, whose West End 'Station' then occupied part of the Nash corner. The clock was placed on an 'island'—then, perhaps more accurately, called a 'rest'—in the centre of the carriageway. Being 'tastefully worked' in a bronzed case and topped by a gilt ball, it was considered by a contemporary reporter to have 'a very elegant appearance'.

Bracket Clocks

Even more varied in style are the many bracket clocks still about. One of the earliest, and certainly one of the most decorative, is that on the old Guildhall in Guildford in Surrey. The hall itself was built in 1682; the clock case was made a year later but its works in 1530. Given its own little gable is an elegant clock that projects from the end gable of a row of 1665 almshouses (built by Sir John Thynne of Longleat) at Longbridge Deverill in Wiltshire. The bracket clock on the tower at St Peter's church at North Hill in Colchester, Essex, used to be on the wall itself, but the unusual earthquake of 1884 so weakened the tower that the clock had to be remounted on a stone bracket.

Although it now bears the cipher of Elizabeth II, the simple clock surmounted by a metal crown that projects from the Post Office in the town square in Falmouth in Cornwall is obviously of Victorian origin. This, like so many such clocks, is well designed, with bold Roman numerals and little extraneous decoration—in contrast to the over-elaborate one in Southampton Street in London, or to the one in Canterbury on the old stone tower of what remains of a church, which, as befits its situation, is topped by a Gothic trefoil decoration.

Many bracket clocks also serve as advertisements for either shops or public houses. Those made to look like enormous pocket watches and usually gilded are obvious advertisements for the watchmaker's shop below. Now painted a jolly red, there is a nice simple square clock with the words 'Noted Wine House' on it hanging over the entrance to the 'Red Lion' in Kilburn High Road in London.

Other bracket clocks carry figures that can have interesting histories. Such a one projects grandly from the ruined church of St Martin-le-Grand in Coney Street in York (Plate 65). It was put up in the seventeenth century and altered in the nineteenth, but its little carved figure of a naval officer taking observations of the

Plate 65 A deliciously Victorian–Gothic bracket supports the 'little admiral' clock which projects from the ruined church of St Martin-le-Grand in Coney Street, York. The eighteenth-century 'admiral' (really of lower rank) is taking observations of the sun with a cross staff (*Author*)

sun with a cross staff, dates from the eighteenth century. Although much restored, he retains a great deal of character; he has been erroneously elevated in rank, locally being affectionately known as the 'Little Admiral'. The church dates from Norman times, when Domesday Book recorded it as being in 'coynge street'. It was much altered over the centuries and, apart from the Lady Chapel, was destroyed in an air raid in 1942. A new church built on the site serves as a memorial to the citizens of York who died in both World Wars. The clock itself survived the disaster and, apart from a new face and repainting, looks much as it did in the nineteenth century.

7 · *Show me the way to go home*

Milestones

Many old milestones have fallen victim to new motorways, new towns, redevelopments and the widening of roads, so that the few that remain are the more precious. Many are often still there, I suspect, only because there is something curious about them, although others remain because some people do appreciate their rarity, beauty or architectural interest. Most are only a few feet high; though a few are of monumental proportions (as well as being monumental in style), such as the 50ft stone obelisk at Chalfont St Peters in Buckinghamshire.

The earliest known milestone or boundary sign is what is called a 'pudding' stone, so named from the fact that its speckled appearance (it consists of flint-like pebbles set in a silica matrix, known geologically as a 'conglomerate') has some resemblance to a plum or Christmas pudding. Usually rather shapeless and tending to narrow towards the top, these stones average 3ft in height and measure about 80in around the base. Some date back to about 5000 BC, when they were used as measuring points or tribal meeting places; the British Museum has dated one, which now rests safely in the yard of the Bull Inn at Nettlebed in Oxfordshire, to about 2000 BC. It is considered to be one of a series that used to stretch from the Thames near Pangbourne in Berkshire to Grimes Graves in Norfolk. Another one in the churchyard of Beauchamp Riding in Holyfield, a village near Waltham Abbey in Essex, is also all that remains of a similar row, which ran between the River Lea to Epping Island at Marks Tey. Now on a pavement in Cookham in Berkshire there is another, the 'Tarry Stone', once used to mark the boundary of Cirencester Abbey and later as a meeting place for local sports, which were held there before 1570.

Some of these pudding stones can be found incorporated into the corner walls of old cottages, such as one at Haddenham in Buckinghamshire; yet others were built into church walls. In Essex there is an example on the south wall of Broomfield church near Chelmsford, and another on the north wall of the church in Magdalen Laver. Also in Essex, at Arkenham, is a Neolithic (2500 to 1500 BC) stone chamber tomb that was later used as a boundary mark or milestone.

Renowned for their efficient road system, it is not surprising that the Romans put up many milestones around their great empire. Most of them are tall, rather narrow columns of rough stone, some with mileages, others carrying only the name of the current Emperor, but most of them bare. In Britain there are still about sixty-six of them, dating from the Occupation (43 to 410 AD). The majority are in museums, a few in situ. Still in its original position is the one that stands near the 73-mile-long Hadrian's Wall (built in the 120s AD) in Northumberland. It stands south of the wall at Stanegate on a Roman road which is still in use. Another example, which is well protected by iron railings, is also in situ at Temple Sowerby in Cumbria. There is another on the A66 road between Corbridge and Carlisle, and in the same county there is a small stone standing on a hillside on the A683. There are a number of 'possible' ones around the country, such as that discovered in 1836 at Sedbergh in Cumbria, near a Roman road. Another, at Bont-du-Merion, 2 miles north-west of Cae Goronwy in Wales, is flat instead of the more usual round shape, and has the distinction of being mentioned in Ogilby's *Britannia* of 1675, one of the oldest books to show route maps. The example at Haddenham in Essex stands on a small grass island near the top of what is now the High Street.

The most famous milestone in Britain must be the one on which Dick (later Sir Richard) Whittington is said to have rested when he heard Bow Bells telling him to return to London to become its lord mayor. Now very well protected by a birdcage-like wrought-iron cover, it is topped by a stone representation of his equally famous cat. It is to be found at the bottom of Highgate Hill in Greater London, and is unlikely to be the original (even if the story is true) as it bears the date 1821. Early in 1977 Islington Council planned to have it removed far from its site to protect it from vandalism, but luckily, at the last moment, discovered that it was listed as a 'building' of historical interest; they could move it only 50yd away and back from the pavement.

Apart from Roman examples, many milestones in England are difficult to date. Until 1773 it was not obligatory to put the mileage on them, or on signposts (both then more accurately referred to as 'direction' posts), but this is no guide, as some early examples do give the mileage. Without this information they are not, of course, true 'mile' stones but purely directional, as they tell the traveller only where he is or where he is going. Apart from the simple slab variety, many of the seventeenth-, eighteenth- and early nineteenth-century stones have elegance and style. With their good Classic proportions and details, and well executed Roman lettering, these are lovely examples of Stuart or Georgian taste. Among the earliest dated examples is a plain stone slab that carries the words 'HERE ENDETH MILE HYWAY. 1667'. Another small

Plate 66 This few-feet-high simple milestone with good Roman lettering is sunk into the pavement on the road to Rye in Kent (*Cressida Pemberton-Pigott*)

stone with a rounded top was put up in 1700 at Withington, a village in Hereford and Worcester; it was made from the shaft of an old cross and gives one the not very useful information that 'THIS IS THE ROAD TO HEREFORD'.

An example of private enterprise concerned with street furniture is the series that was set up between Cambridge and Barkway in Hertfordshire about 1725 by the Fellows of Trinity Hall at the university, whose arms the stone bears. Alas, only one is left, at Barkway. Another stone on the Oxford Road, called a 'shy' milestone, dates from 1732 and gets its name from the fact that it gives only the barest cryptic information. Unless in the know, one is unaware that 'The City' means London, 'The Country Town' refers to Aylesbury and 'The University' is Oxford. It is also 'shy' because of its position high up on the wall, though it could be easily read by coachmen or those on horseback. A similarly high stone is to be found at Dorchester in Dorset, giving the distance to Hyde Park, which was for long the measuring point to London. At this point stands Apsley House, the 1st Duke of Wellington's mansion, which used to be called 'Number One, London'. (Distances to London are now measured to the Charles I statue in Trafalgar Square.) A 1737 milestone made in the form of a triangular seat was useful for those waiting for the stagecoach; it was positioned in 1801 to stand on the outskirts of Bradford in West Yorkshire. One side carries a moulded hand pointing to Denholme Gate and the other a hand pointing to Brickhouse. As it lies between Cormersal and Haworth, it must often have been passed by the Brontë sisters, who were frequent visitors to friends at the Red House in Cormersal.

A square brick pillar resembling a gate-post at a crossroads near the village of Otterton in Devon was put up in 1743, and gives four sets of directions in biblical phrases. Another rather heavy stone pillar, topped by a foliated ball and probably eighteenth-century, at Holt in Norfolk is unusual in that it gives the distances to nearby country 'seats', the most important being Holkham Hall, a Palladian mansion built between 1734 and 1759. Another square stone pillar with a small dome on top stands between the gates of Sheffield Park in East Sussex, about 12 miles from Brighton. It is of interest because it gives the early name for this town, when it was only a fishing village—Brighthelmstone. The same spelling is to be found on an oblong stone set into the wall of a timber-framed bookshop in the High Street in Lewes, in the same county. In fine Roman lettering it tells the traveller that he is only 8 miles from Brighthelmstone, 50 from 'The Standard' (an inn or public house) in Cornhill and 49 from Westminster Bridge—unhelpfully omitting the fact that both these places are in London. Well protected by iron railings is a square pillar topped by a small spire and a ball which stands between two busy carriageways on the Great North Road at Alconbury Hill in Cambridgeshire. This one gives mileage, as does the 1752 round column, topped by a ball and called 'The Pedestal' which was put up outside East Wycombe in Buckinghamshire some time in the eighteenth century.

A lovely round pillar known locally as the 'White Lady' was erected in 1767 on the London road at Esher in Surrey; and West Wycombe boasts four fine stone milestones in the shape of columns topped by balls. On the Aylesbury road there is a large oblong stone, one side showing 'THAME' in large Roman capitals, '*Aylesbury*' in small italic letters, and 'Miles $9\frac{1}{2}$'; its reverse is decorated with a well carved pointing hand.

The 1766 small flat pediment-shaped stone $2\frac{1}{2}$ miles north of Shaftesbury in Dorset is confusing because it informs the traveller that he is 11 miles from Shaston which no longer exists, it being the old name for this town. More a question of abbreviation than alteration is the wording on an undated small square milestone in the New Forest in Hampshire. The wording is engraved on a metal plaque, Christchurch being rendered as 'x i CHURCH' and Bournemouth shortened to 'BOURNE'. There are several flat pointed stones around the area of East Hoathly in East Sussex that are the ultimate in obscurity: they carry a rebus composed of a family insignia (a series of bows topped by a bell and a number), one, called the 'Pelham Buckle', carrying 50 and the other, with the badge of the Pelham family on it, 53. All is understood when one realises that these stones show the number of miles to St Mary-le-Bow church (renowned for its bells) in Cheapside, London.

With all this individuality, divergence and vagueness, it is understandable that by the middle of the eighteenth century the Government felt it necessary to pass legislation to clarify matters for the increasing number of road travellers. Attention was centred on the system of turnpike roads that already covered a great deal of the country. These roads were barred at intervals with a series of gates—two cross-bars on pikes, turning on a post: hence turnpike —and a toll house at which a fee was paid. This system lasted well into the nineteenth century, and exists on certain bridges today. During the eighteenth century there were about 4,000 turnpike trusts, which must have made travelling an expensive business, as each charged a fee for its particular stretch of road, which could vary from a few to many miles in length. The tolls collected were supposed to be spent on the upkeep of the roads, but many fraudulent trusts kept the money for themselves. The Turnpike Act of 1767 pointed out that 'the laws for the general Regulation of the Turnpike Roads of this Kingdom are very numerous and in some respects Ineffectual'. It was therefore decided to repeal them and pass one law 'for carrying such Purposes into Execution'.

Although this did something to alleviate abuses, it was not until 1773 that the General Turnpike Act was passed, giving the Government greater powers. Under it a surveyor for each trust was impelled to 'cause to be fixed, in the most convenient Place where . . . Ways meet, a Stone or Post with an inscription thereon in Large Letters, containing the Name of, and Distances from, the next Market Town or Towns, or other considerable Places or Place to which the said Highways respectively lead'. The surveyor was also directed to put up flood-warning signs and show the best routes through flooded roads. If after 3 months of being given these instructions he continued to ignore them, he was liable to a fine of 20 shillings (£1).

As has already been pointed out, dated and undated stones were put up before this Act, but it is safe to say that the majority of such stones or posts date from about 1773. From the middle of the eighteenth century to the early nineteenth century, with Neo-Classicism all the rage, the obelisk was a favourite shape for milestones. One of the grandest is that now standing outside the Imperial War Museum in St George's Road, SE1, in London. Made of blocks of stone, it is 39ft 8in high, on a 6in concrete base. It used to stand in the centre of nearby St George's Circus, where it was known as 'The Obelisk'. When the idea for it was mooted in 1770, it was feared that it would be a traffic hazard even though it then stood in St George's Fields, when they were fields. To still this criticism, when the obelisk was finished in 1771, it was fitted with bracket lamps at each corner. These lamps have a strange history. In a later print they have become separate lamp-posts, but a photograph of c1905 shows them fixed to the stone once more, and yet another photograph, apparently taken just before the obelisk's removal, shows the lamps again as separate posts.

In 1905 it was decided to remove the stone to make way for a clock tower (see p 108), which in its turn was removed in 1937. In 1907 the obelisk then stood outside the old Bethlehem or Bedlam, a mental hospital, which was demolished in the early 1860s to make way for the erection of the Imperial War Museum in 1868–9. When the stone was finally resited, it was lampless, the lamps being of no use in its new position by the side of the road.

Fine Roman letters and numerals are carved in the stone, one side carrying the date and the name of the then lord mayor, and the others pedantically precise directions. One reads ONE MILE FROM PALACE YARD, WESTMINSTER HALL, another ONE MILE XXXX FEET FROM LONDON BRIDGE, and the third ONE MILE CCI FEET FROM FLEET STREET. These measurements are now meaningless, as the obelisk is no longer in its original position; it would seem sensible to return it to its home (now a rough grass circle), when its measurements would again make sense.

There is a similar but much smaller obelisk milestone on the bridge at Richmond in Greater London, and another at Brampton in Cambridgeshire that is topped by a ball. The 1808 one at Bredon in Hereford and Worcester is broken three-quarters way up and has a small shelf. One of the most famous of obelisks, and in little danger of vanishing, as it now stands in the window of Barclay's Bank in the Edgware Road in London, is the Tyburn Stone. This originally stood half a mile away opposite the present junction of Star Street and Edgware Road at the Tyburn Turnpike House, which, with its three gates, stood from 1760–1829 at the junction of Oxford Street, Bayswater Road and Edgware Road. The stone previously marked the spot where public hangings took place from 1196 to 1783. In 1884 it was preserved by Consolidated London Properties Limited, who presented it to the London County Council in 1909, when, with the consent of the Capital and Counties Bank Limited, it was re-erected in its present position. The wording is much worn and one can only just distinguish the words 'TYBURNE GATE'.

The following examples only go to prove that if the more ordinary milestones are vanishing, the English, with their passion for the eccentric, are allowing many oddities to survive. One can only hope that this trait will not disappear in less tolerant, less interested and less imaginative future generations. Despite this endearing trait, however, only one is left of a series of fine large obelisk milestones called 'The Gout Track'. It stands in the High Street in Marlow in Buckinghamshire, and was one of the milestones erected by the Cecil family of Hatfield House in Hertfordshire, which, like so many over-indulging aristocrats of the eighteenth and nineteenth centuries, suffered from gout and frequently went to Bath to take its curative waters. To avoid London the route ran through Amersham, Wycombe, Marlow and Henley to join the Bath road at Reading. Hence the stones, and the fact that the turnpike trust along this road was the richer by £2,000 a year between 1822 and 1834.

In 1834 Thomas Telford died, aged 77. A Scottish engineer, he was responsible among other things for a bridge over the Severn, the Menai Suspension Bridge, the Caledonian and Ellesmere canals, many docks and roads—and the milestones that are now named after him. Flat and pointed, they look rather like tombstones. Two of the simplest are found in Wales: one (line by line) reads 'HOLY-/HEAD,/40/C. CURIG/5 Furlongs/CERNIOGE/13m—6f'; and a similar one on the A5 in Anglesey reads 'HOLY-/HEAD/21/MONA/8/ BANGOR/4', Mona being a former coaching inn between Holyhead and Bangor. Rather grander is the Telford stone at Shrewsbury in Salop, which tells the traveller that he is 150 miles from London.

As the century progressed, the Gothic style became more fashionable and a Gothic spire (now carefully railed round) was put up at Fairmile, Devonshire, in 1871 in memory of Bishop John Patterson, who was killed by 'savages' in foreign parts. Also very Victorian Gothic is the mausoleum-like stone at Newbold-on-Stour in Warwickshire (Plate 67) which bears the following rather proud and touching verse:

Plate 67 Although dated 1911 this cast-iron milestone is typically Victorian in style. Outside the Royal Geographical Society in Knightsbridge, London (*Mansell Collection*)

6 miles
To Shakespeare's Tomb whose Name
Is known throughout the Earth
To Shipston 4 whose Lesser Fame
Boasts no such Poet's Birth.

The Victorians made a number of cast-iron milestones that were usually triangular with a sloping top (Plate 67). Most, as in this example, carried pointing hands and are quite large. They are usually black on white although there is an unusual example of the reverse in County Durham, giving the information that one is

Plate 68 A crude milestone with a cast-iron plaque fastened to a mounting block made from a single piece of stone instead of the usual separate steps. North Cave, near Hull, Humberside (*Geoffrey N. Wright*)

Plate 69 A typical tomb-like Victorian milestone with rhyming directions. Newbold-on-Stour, Warwickshire (*Rosemary Atherton*)

7 miles from 'Lanchester' and two from 'Wolsincham'. The one at Chatteris in Cambridgeshire carries a pair of crossed keys, and that between Leicester and Coventry is placed exactly 12 miles between them. A similar one at Atherstone in Warwickshire, which stands outside the 'Olde Red Lion' hotel, once proclaimed that it was 100 miles from London, Liverpool and Lincoln; a set of distances later discovered to be incorrect. The one at Thirsk in North Yorkshire is a memorial to a local drover, one side bearing a crude representation of the man himself and the other an equally crude bull. As an example of a flat iron milestone the one at Barton Parish registers the fact that the traveller is 4 miles from Cambridge.

Particularly idiosyncratic is the 1801 mile 'stone' built into the wall over a fishpond at Matlock in Derbyshire, for although at one time it may have been so, it is now no longer visible from the road.

Duty Posts

Many people living in the Home Counties must be puzzled by a number of low milestone-like posts carrying the arms of the City of London and some numbers, which are to be found in a 20 to 25 mile radius of the capital. These are wine or coal duty posts and the reason for them dates from the seventeenth century. The earliest, now gone, were put up after the Great Fire of London in 1666 by the Corporation of London, which was the official supervisor of goods entering the Thames. Among other tasks it undertook to measure the amounts of coal and wine brought into the Port of London, but finding itself in financial difficulties following the Great Fire, decided to add a coal and wine tax.

At first this tax provided a good income, but in the eighteenth century the transport of coal and wine moved from the land to the sea, and the tax was more difficult to collect. It was consequently decided to erect posts at points outside the capital where the duty was to be paid. The first posts were wooden, but later ones were made of iron or stone (the ones we now see), and at one time there were over 250 of them. The present number is not recorded, but in 1965 fifty-four were listed in Surrey alone. The posts began to become obsolete when Acts relating to goods being recorded entering London were abolished in 1889, and completely so when, 2 years later, the Corporation relinquished its right to collect tolls and act as measurer and weigher.

Signposts

'One good thing in most parts of this principality', wrote Celia Fiennes when riding across Lancashire in 1698, '[is] that at all cross wayes there are Posts with Hands pointing to each road with the names of the great town or market towns that it leads to', proving that at this time such signs were a welcome rarity. However, although now much restored, there is a post that is said to date from 1201 at Basset's Pole in Staffordshire. It stands at the intersection of the A446 and A453 between Sutton Coldfield and Tamworth, and is now a Victorian iron pole with small bollards at each corner. Another restored example can be found at Teddington Hands in Gloucestershire, just east of Tewkesbury, in the form of a stone column surmounted by a ball that in its turn is topped by a spire; the whole is surrounded by a low brick wall. It was put up by one Edward Attwood in the seventeenth century but repaired by a descendant, Alice Attwood, in 1876.

Still much in its original condition is the 1669 signpost at the crossroads just beyond the top of Broadway Hill in Worcestershire.

Plate 70 This hefty column of a signpost with nicely pierced 'arms' was put up in 1800 and restored in 1929. Little Brampton, near Ludlow, Salop (*Geoffrey N. Wright*)

It was erected by a local farmer with the Dickensian name of Nathan Izod. Its wooden post carries four metal arms that terminate in hands (a type appropriately referred to then as a 'handing' post) which point to Worcester, Gloucester, Cheltenham and Oxford. There is a nice wooden post, with a ribbed section where the arms meet, which was put up in 1777 at Brownhill in Staffordshire; in line with the 1773 Act it shows proper mileages. Considered to be one of the most elegant of signposts, and now officially preserved, is that at the 'Three Lamps' junction outside Bristol. Made of iron, it is in the shape of an Ionic column, with part of a classical frieze across the top surmounted by a Roman-style figure. 'BATH' and 'WELLS' are nicely lettered in Roman style pierced in the iron, and each arm is finished with a hand. A nice hefty column of a signpost with metal pierced arms was put up at Little Brampton near Ludlow, Salop, about 1800 (Plate 70).

There are two particularly interesting signposts in Warwickshire. One is a wooden post with metal-handed 'arms' and topped by the flat iron representation of a bear holding a ragged post or staff; this used to be the crest of the Dudley family (who became Earls of Leicester, the most famous being the first, Queen Elizabeth's favourite) but are now the arms of the county of Warwick, where the first Earl owned the now ruined but magnificent Kenilworth castle. The other is an elaborate twirly affair at Norton Lindsey, Warwickshire, which was put up to celebrate Queen Victoria's Diamond Jubilee of 1897 (Plate 71).

Looking like a very ornate pillar box—round with cast-iron decorations and with a 'fish-scale' dome—is the signpost at Breadsall in Derbyshire. Of uncertain date is the one at Newbrough in Northumberland, where the designer has taken 'Cross

Plate 71 An eccentric stone and twirly iron signpost put up to celebrate Queen Victoria's 1897 Jubilee. Norton Lindsey, Warwickshire (*Rosemary Atherton*)

Plate 72 An imaginative interpretation of a necessary direction which takes the form of a St Andrew's cross. Newbrough, Northumberland (*Barbara Denness*)

Roads' literally and portrayed a St Andrew's cross (Plate 72). Directional signs to places of interest in towns and villages can be fascinating: mounted on a floridly executed iron lamp-post base in Bath is a sign on an equally twirly bracket pointing the way to the 'Hot Springs and Roman Baths'. Of the many signs pointing to the nearest public lavatories, and of curiosity value, is the one in the village green at Staindrop in County Durham, which is fastened to a broken-off column that was probably once a lamp-post standard. Now very unusual is any sign using the word 'Urinal', though two point the way to a very dilapidated brick and tiled 'Gentlemens' on the Victoria Park Road in Hackney in London (Plate 73).

Plague Stones

Many people may be intrigued by what look like enormous stone bird-baths or toadstools standing on the sides of roads or isolated in gardens. Most of these are what are called plague stones. They are most probably made from old millstones and were a useful piece of street furniture when all sorts of pestilence ravaged this country from the Middle Ages well into the nineteenth century—although these stones were probably not much used after the seventeenth century.

They were placed outside towns so that at times of plague the less affected country people could bring in food for the stricken townspeople and leave it at this spot. As it was too risky for the well to meet the sick, the infected victims left their payment of coins in the hollow in the centre of the stone; for further 'protection' this dip was filled with vinegar, which was thought to be a disinfectant.

There are not many of these stones left, although many may exist unrecognised. The one outside Bury St Edmunds in Suffolk stands at Risbygate Street at the corner of Chalk Road, where a market used to be held (Plate 74). Although it could be earlier, the stone is said to date from 1636, when bubonic plague ravaged the city. The one in Leeds, looking very like a mushroom as it stands on a rough plinth, has had a modern '1666, Plague' written on it in white paint, while the example at Penrith in Cumbria is known to date from about 1630. This one is made of a deepish brown stone and is probably no longer in situ, as it stands in a garden—

Plate 73 A rare urinal sign, one of a pair in Victoria Park Road, Hackney, London E9 (*Ivan Radley*)

Plate 74 A plague stone, probably made from old millstones. The hollow was for vinegar-disinfected money with which the victims paid the townspeople who left food for them at this spot. Out-Risby-Gate, Bury St Edmunds Suffolk (*Barbara Denness*)

unless the garden has subsequently been made around it. The stone at Newport on the Cambridge Road in Essex is a very rough, rather shapeless mass. As it stands near the site of an old leper hospital, it is referred to as a leper stone, but served the same sort of function as a plague stone. The one at Croewylen at Oswestry in Salop commemorates a plague of 1559 and is made from the base of an old market cross. The stone at Derby in the Arboretum (or special area for trees) is a rather more sophisticated affair, as it consists of two squared-off granite blocks mounted on three steps—which are probably of a much later date.

Bollards

Dr Johnson is said to have touched bollards for luck. Today, although he would find few left from his day, there are still a surprising number of later examples around that would allow him to indulge in this particular superstition. This is largely because bollards (also called stumps or carriage posts) still often serve their original purpose of barring traffic in small roads, lanes, cul-de-sacs and under colonnades; protecting 'islands' or statues; marking parking places outside churches, public houses and large buildings; and preventing parking on stretches of pavement.

Dr Johnson died in 1784, but the majority of bollards date from the Napoleonic Wars and later. The ones from these wars are, in fact, a range of different sized cannon muzzles, their ends filled in by small domes. At the time of the Battle of Trafalgar, 1805, the Carron Company of Falkirk in Scotland had a virtual monopoly of the making of the short light naval cannons carried on the upper decks of warships—they were even often referred to as 'carronades' in honour of the company. But when the wars were over, with the Battle of Waterloo in 1815, this company naturally feared that there would be less need for their guns, and that the government would also make use of the great number of captured French and Spanish pieces. The company pointed this out and it was agreed that a large number of the captured guns would be sold off—to be made into bollards. This is why several thousand suddenly appeared, mostly in London streets.

They range from the narrow to the comparatively bulky, but all have an elegance about them. Many are marked with embossed parish names and borough arms or dates (Plate 75). One marked 'Anne' (the Parish of St Anne and not, as one might think, referring to the Queen of that name, which would make it much earlier) and dated 1832 is one of many still standing in Covent Garden, London. An attempt has recently been made to reproduce this style in concrete in the Waterloo Road in Southwark, but owing to the fragility of this material compared with the strength of the original iron, these are already showing signs of wear.

Among those not made of cannons, the most elegant are the ones

Plate 75 A typical boliard—painted silver—made from a Napoleonic Wars' cannon. In the Parish of St James' Westminster, at the corner of Brewer Street, London W1 (*Author*)

put up during the reign of William IV (1830–7), which are flat, ribbed and pointed (Plate 76). Some carry the monarch's cipher, and many plain ones are either later or modern copies. There are two exceptionally sturdy but fine ribbed bollards on the pavement in Stamford Street in Southwark outside the London Nautical School, a Neo-classic building dating from 1826—a perfect example of street furniture fitting the building against which it stands.

There is considerably more variety among later Victorian designs, from the Gothic to the happy-go-lucky mixture of styles so beloved of this period. Still with a Regency elegance about them, although they are rather heavy and coarse, are the octagonal ones

Plate 76 An elegant William IV (1830–7) cast-iron bollard. finely shaped and decorated. Lower Regent Street, London SW1 (*Author*)

Plate 77 A pair of Victorian 'Norman' style bollards put to good use in Albert Square, Whitehaven, Cumbria (*Barbara Denness*)

often embellished with raised stars. Those outside the monstrously Victorian Gothic St Pancras Hotel in London are Gothic to match. For other Victorian examples see Plates 77–9.

Probably quite early, and surprisingly still surviving, are simple wooden bollards. For some reason they are generally to be found outside churches or cathedrals, and are often slender and nicely ribbed, such as those at Penrith in Cumbria. Similar ones are to be found in such places as Wells, Warwick and Cambridge, although it is by no means the rule that an old town or city will have any. Mention of Cambridge reminds me that there is a strange little row of eight low iron bollards linked with chains (a common feature, except that in many cases the chains are now missing) outside King's College. Above them is a plaque carrying the following information: 'This piece of land encircled by bollards

Plate 78 A series of pleasantly shaped cucumber-like bollards, Whitehaven, Cumbria (*Barbara Denness*)

and chains is the property of the Chancellor, Members and Scholars of the University of Cambridge.' This bollarded area is so small that one wonders why it was considered important and useful, but at least the plaque does something to ensure that the bollards will not be removed.

Although many old bollards remain in such rows, as many stand in dignified isolation; or a single one (perhaps askew or sinking into the ground) will be left among modern ones—an aloof old aristocrat ignoring its feeble concrete or thin iron social inferiors. Sometimes this mixture can be visually unfortunate and unpleasing; for much as one applauds the preservation of the old, it is often achieved at the expense of artistic symmetry. In Queen Square off Russell Street in London a nice 1840s iron pump is surrounded by four protective bollards, but unfortunately only two of the original Gothic-style bollards remain, the missing ones having been replaced by plain modern concrete examples. The imbalance is all too striking and uncomfortable. Much better, I feel, to have either copied the originals (here the matter of expense is an obvious and understandable objection) or to have removed (removed, not destroyed) them to another site and substituted only modern examples.

Although so many bollards of all descriptions are still left, one has only to study turn-of-the-century photographs to realise how many more have vanished. Where once most 'islands' sported at least four, now there are none, or a remaining one has been turned into a 'Keep Left' sign or such signs have replaced bollards altogether. It would take up too much space to enumerate all the

Plate 79 Four iron bollards and the base of an old lamp-post bar the way to a cul-de-sac in Hexham, Northumberland (*Barbara Denness*)

examples of decimation, but in London alone most main thorough-fares are almost denuded.

There is an unusual explanation of the fate of some of these. A Londoner visiting the Swanage area of Dorset would be surprised to see so many cannon bollards from his home city forming gate-posts. They come from such parishes or districts as St James, Westminster, St Giles, Bloomsbury, St Anne's, St Martin's (1822), Middlesex (1819), and Clerkenwell—the last being marked 'Alex Wright Thos. Partridge', churchwarden of the parish in 1862. The reason that these bollards are so far from home and performing another useful function lies in the fact that in the nineteenth century a firm of building contractors, Mowlem & Butt, did business in both London and Dorset. Their ships carried Purbeck stone to London and on the return needed ballast; what better, it was discovered, than bollards, which were being removed from a London already experiencing great alterations. On reaching Dorset it seemed a waste to throw these bollards away; hence their present use.

Bollards with rings on them were also used as tethering or hitching posts for horses, like the one with two rings on it in the main street at Market Harborough in Leicestershire. Some were given horses' head finials. There is one of these at Drewsteignton in Devon, which appears to have been copied from an 1870s French iron-caster's catalogue.

Most iron bollards nowadays are painted white, black or silver, though some still retain their wide horizontal black and white stripes, which were applied in the early 1960s. During World War II bollards were painted white so that they could be seen in the black-out.

Many bollards are fastened to gateways or entrances to buildings, where they protect the walls from the damage that could be caused by carriage or cart wheels taking the corner at too great a lick. Some of these are of classic shape (Plate 80), and others merely rounded posts or rather shapeless mounds.

Recently Camden Council in London has actually put up a row of twenty-four old iron bollards in Belsize Road and some in Greville Place. Leicester Square in London used to boast half-a-dozen silver-painted sturdy Victorian bollards bearing the arms of the City of Westminster. But when, in 1971, the square was turned into a rather badly designed 'piazza', many more of these bollards were copied and placed in close rows to break up the walking area. To mark the Queen's Silver Jubilee in 1977, the bollards were painted black and white with the arms in red. The Department of the Environment has also made bollards from old moulds for other places in London and Ironbridge in Salop. Admirable though this may be, to my mind it is a somewhat retrograde step. Preservation of the old is one thing; pastiche or artificial re-creation is

Plate 80 One of the many bollards which protect the corners of doorways opening into yards; this one is at Carlisle, Cumbria (*Barbara Denness*)

another. We are living in the 1970s and, however much we may deplore it, I feel that a bollard put up now should be of this period, so long as it has been well designed and made of a lasting material, and that attention is paid to the fact that it must fit in with its surroundings.

Warning Signs

With the increase of road traffic in the 1860s it became necessary to add more warning signs than those for floods, advocated in the 1773 Turnpike Act. These signs have now proliferated so much that many posts are a mass of bewildering and often contradictory, as well as often unconsciously funny, warnings and directions. The 1860s saw signs put up on bridges warning the drivers of heavy vehicles that they ran the risk of causing the bridge to collapse if they drove on to it. In the 1870s, when cycling was all the rage, it was important to put up warning signs at the top of steep hills, as these early machines had either poor brakes or none at all. By the early years of this century signs were needed for the drivers of motorcars. At first only words were used but after World War I they were accompanied, or replaced, by symbols. Such symbols on the Continent were already standardised but, as with so much else in Britain, individualistic signs continued to be used and it was not until 1964 that this country fell into line with European usage. A reminder of the not-so-distant past are the few signs that still warn travellers to beware of horses.

Plate 81 An amusing sign which really warns the driver to anticipate a ramp ahead; put there to slow down traffic on a dangerous part of the road outside Rushbrooke, Suffolk (*Barbara Denness*)

There are countless unconsciously amusing signs. One at Padstow in Cornwall appears to direct people to public conveniences in the sea, while a sign painted on a wall in Lewes tells cattle and calves to turn right but pigs to go straight on. At St Just in Cornwall, on a very decorative iron post, a sign points to the church and the bar, emphasising the age-long practice of building the public house as near as possible to the place of worship. 'Dead slow. Sleeping policeman' outside Rushbrooke in Suffolk sounds like something out of 'Monty Python', but in fact refers to the fact that on lonely roads the driver must expect a ramp, which is there to slow down traffic in the absence of a real policeman (Plate 81). (A fine collection of such signs, both sensible and amusing, is now on view at the National Motor Museum at Beaulieu in Hampshire).

Many signs mounted on ornate iron columns can still be found standing on pavements outside shops and public houses. In Abbey Road in London NW8 there are two such: one says 'Chemist', which lights up, and the other is for a grocer's. Some post offices are also signposted in this way, the signs displayed on poles or fixed to the top of pillar boxes.

Street Names

Essential to finding one's way in an urban area, of course, are street names. The most sophisticated form is for names to be carved into the buildings themselves. The best example of this is the series in Bath where the names, beautifully executed in Roman lettering, are believed to be the work of one stonemason about 1730, a good example of a necessary ancillary being made an integral part of the building.

Early names were only painted on the walls, and in many places one can still see traces of this, often alongside later, more durable iron or tile versions. Although many of these have been replaced by modern characterless uniform plain iron slabs, some of the old, more imaginative and varying signs still exist. Certainly each village, and usually each district in a big city has (or had) its own particular design, owing to the fact that the job was usually handed to a local blacksmith, tile-maker or foundry.

Most old cast-iron signs are long and narrow with a raised border and the name in raised capital letters. Some ends are rounded, some square; while yet others have a scoop taken out of the corners. The most elaborate are finished at either end with a fancy scroll or shell (Plate 82). The majority of iron signs needed only a few screws, but the tiled ones must have taken much more time and trouble to put up (Plate 83). As well as disappearing from streets

Plate 82 A fine cast-iron street sign with nicely executed lettering and shell-patterned ends. A design which occurs throughout the village of Brampton in Cumbria (*Barbara Denness*)

Plate 83 This black-and-white tiled street sign is typical of North London (*Author*). In Devon the same kind of tiles are blue.

when they are demolished or when the local council feels the time has come to make the area look more 'modern', many iron signs fall victim to those who think it smart to have such a sign hanging on the walls of their rooms. But some are stolen for quite another reason. When the Beatles released the record 'Abbey Road' in November 1969, the signs in this particular thoroughfare in London's St John's Wood began to disappear, stolen as souvenirs by dedicated fans. No sooner did Westminster City Council replace the signs than they were again removed. Even a particularly strong new screw being no obstacle to the really determined. A very fine example on the corner of Abbey Road and Blenheim Terrace lasted only one and a half days, and Abbey Road soon became the only long unnamed road in London. It was suggested to the authorities that they resorted to the old practice of painting the names, as not even fanatics would be likely to remove whole walls, but the suggestion was not taken up. By the end of 1975, however, the fans' ardour had cooled, for the road is identifiable once more.

House and Shop Numbers

Of equal importance to street names is the numbering of buildings. Here again painting was, and to a large extent still is, a favoured method. One finds numbers painted on the fanlights over the front doors of eighteenth- and nineteenth-century houses, on their gateposts or walls, and more often on the facias of shops. Some are executed in good Roman or Arabic numerals, others in florid Victorian curves (these mainly now confined to old shops) while yet others are crude, to say the least.

More numerous are iron numbers screwed to the door. Here one has to be rather careful as to dating, for some modern firms have produced good Classic numerals, which one finds attached appropriately to eighteenth-century houses as well as to those of later periods. Other numerals, and these are getting rare, are painted on enamel plaques fastened either to the door or on the wall next to it. There are also a number of more ornate versions where the numerals are cut out of metal on either hanging plaques or on lamp-post-like lanterns.

Cabbies' Shelters

One of the most popular ways of getting home in the nineteenth century was by Hansom cab. Although this vehicle has long vanished from our streets, some of the many shelters put up for cabmen still remain. They are one of the few relics of the horse age to survive and still be of use, even if the cabs are now motorised. Alas, in 1976 the Taxi Drivers' Association lamented that out of an original 100 or so, only eight remained in central London (Plate 84).

The first two-wheeled horse-drawn Hansom cabs appeared in

Plate 84 A well lit and comfortable cottage-looking cabby shelter (with a fine three-branched lamp-post and bollards) drawn in 1901. Nowadays the few shelters which are left are often in a disgraceful state of disrepair (*Tony Grubhoper*)

London in 1834. Apart from the sedan chairs, and stagecoaches for long distances, they were the first means of public transport, and soon came to be called 'indispensable accessories to a railway journey of such a length to demand luggage'; they were also used for business errands, to save time and, in the evenings, to reach 'opportunities of social intercourse', and return home afterwards. By 1888 there were 7,396 licensed cabs and 15,514 cabmen in London alone. (In 1896 there were 7,585 Hansoms and 3,449 four-wheelers.) As with other amenities, the capital was surprisingly slow in providing any shelter for this important work-force. Experimental shelters were first tried out in Liverpool about 1870, and Glasgow and Birmingham followed suit, but it was not until January 1875 that they appeared in the London streets.

They were wooden structures, painted green and usually made to look like miniature cottages, with wooden or slate pitched roofs, little gables and a central turret through which the fumes from the stove could escape. This stove was for warmth and for heating up refreshments, which were sold 'at a fair price'. There was often also a supply of books and papers with which cabbies could while away their waiting time. An engraving of 1875 called 'Newly erected shelter and refreshment-house for Cab-men' shows a typical interior: cabbies sit around reading, smoking long clay pipes, and drinking from cups while a large coffee pot boils on the stove. In 1889 these shelters were described as being of 'different models and sizes' but those of 'later construction' were 'decidedly ornamental to the streets, being elegant in design and often prettily decorated'. It is these that are mostly still with us, although often in a disgraceful state of repair even though much used. The one in Leicester Square was given in 1901 by Sir Squire Bancroft, a grateful user of cabs.

Cab shelters are among the pieces of street furniture to which people have become strangely attached. Even as early as May 1893, when it was found necessary in Ipswich in Suffolk to remove a particularly lavish shelter, with arched latticed windows, rather than demolish it, it was put on a large flat cart and drawn by the corporation steam roller and reinstated in the local park. Much later in 1974, when the Howard Hotel, a plate-glass building, was put up at the Temple in London, its owners wanted the old cabbies' shelter outside it to be removed as they felt it not to be in keeping with their smart new image; but they met with strong local opposition. As a compromise, the shelter was moved further down the road. Another shelter in London has taken a similar trip. It used to stand in the Brompton Road not far from the Victoria and Albert Museum, next to an iron-railinged pair of underground public lavatories. When, early in 1976, the latter were demolished, because of new roadworks, the shelter was moved a few hundred yards down the road nearer the Museum. One day it may well find itself inside.

Porters' Rests

As a porters' rest is such a useful piece of street furniture, it is surprising that there appears to be only one of them now in existence. Standing at the Hyde Park end of Piccadilly in London, it consists of a 3in wooden plank that stands on two high cast-iron columns. Although it is reputed to have been used solely as a resting place for coffins on the way to the churchyard, the more likely explanation is that outlined on the plaque, which now runs along it and reads as follows: 'This porters' rest was erected in 1861 by the Vestry of St George Hanover Square for the benefit of porters and others carrying burdens, as a relic of a past period in London's history. It is hoped that the people will aid in its preservation.' This hope has, up to now, been fulfilled, even though there were fears that the 'rest' would vanish when extensive alterations were made to Hyde Park Corner in the late 1950s.

Seats and Benches

Most people on a long walk, whether taken for pleasure or from necessity, feel in need of a 'good sit down'. One such walker at the turn of this century was obviously so put out at not finding a suitable seat that she had a plain wooden one put up on the esplanade at Ryde, Isle of Wight. It carries the following simple inscription:

'Rested. Remember Winnie Bowers.' Many since have had cause to do just that.

The inscription on an earlier stone seat expresses much the same sentiment, although it is overlaid with another meaning. It is to be found in Burley Street in Hampshire, and is also a direction stone, as it reads: 'To Ringwood', which bald statement is followed by the words: 'Rest and be thankful'. But tired walkers were to be thankful not only for the rest but because an inscription carries the following words: 'PEACE restored 27th March 1802', this being one of the breaks in the long Napoleonic wars.

Apart from low walls, the odd fallen tree trunk and the steps at the feet of market crosses, there was precious little to ease the traveller in the Middle Ages. Most of the older seats still with us date from the nineteenth century but alas, many of them, although still much used, are sadly neglected, with rotting boards and cast-iron frames rusted and/or broken. Unlike even remote villages on the Continent, the British seem not to have gone in for the custom of putting little stone seats outside houses in the street. Such foreign seats usually blend in well with the architecture, but British ones tend to look out of place. Now looking incongruous, but once very much part of its surroundings, is a large stone alcove with a seat in it now standing in Victoria Park in London's Hackney. It is the only remaining seat from old London Bridge, which was demolished in 1832.

By the middle of the nineteenth century local councils and private people began to pay for seats and benches to be installed in streets, parks and on esplanades. Although serviceable, the plain wooden ones on simple iron frames are of no great visual

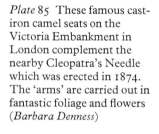

Plate 85 These famous cast-iron camel seats on the Victoria Embankment in London complement the nearby Cleopatra's Needle which was erected in 1874. The 'arms' are carried out in fantastic foliage and flowers (*Barbara Denness*)

interest; more in need of preservation are the diminishing number of fanciful cast-iron framed ones that proliferated in the Victorian and Edwardian eras. With these, as with so much else, designers really let themselves go with every conceivable style. A particular feature of such frames is the use of animal and plant forms, examples of the naturalistic school of design which, beginning in the 1840s, flowered into the Art Nouveau style of the last years of the nineteenth century and the early years of this. Indeed, some of the designs border on the Surrealistic school of the 1920s.

Plate 86 At first sight the frame of this Victorian bench appears to be made of real branches but they are, in fact, cast iron. Hexham, Northumberland (*Barbara Denness*)

Plate 87 Cast-iron snakes curl in an Art Nouveau frame to support this bench: an example of imaginative design rarely encountered today. Seahouses, Northumberland (*Barbara Denness*)

135

The most famous of this type—and ones that will not, one hopes, vanish yet awhile—is the series of extraordinary benches lining the Victoria Embankment in London. When the so-called 'Cleopatra's Needle' obelisk was put up there in 1874, it inspired the firm of Albion Ironworks of Westminster to make the benches, which are supported either by sphinxes or crouching camels (Plate 85). These are rare and extreme examples of the genre, but many humbler benches were given bizarre if less exotic and often less relevant frames. There are benches that look as if they are supported by branches of trees until one realises that they are made of cast iron (Plate 86). A more elaborate example of 'nature' is one carrying a squirrel improbably eating grapes; this seat is in Bullgill, a village near Aspatria in Cumbria, which used to have a number of them but has now only one, the rest having been victims of vandalism. Snakes lend themselves to forming bench frames, and many iron ones curve in an Art Nouveau manner (Plate 87). Yet others are made in the form of much enlarged plants such as vines and blackberries. Much simpler are the sturdy no-nonsense granite and concrete benches to be found in Wales, Cornwall and Devon.

8 · Step on it

Gratings and Covers

In 1905, Haward's, advertising in *The Ironmonger Diary and Text Book*, was proud to announce its 'Semi-Prism' pavements lights, which could be used to convert underground rooms into 'valuable business premises'. These lights are only one of the pieces of street furniture which (probably without realising it) we tread on every day. Others underfoot include gratings and gutters—in the iron-mongery trade also known as gulley frames, weirs and sough grates—ventilation holes and pavement lights, as well as manhole and inspection covers of all descriptions, most dating from the time when roads became 'made-up' during the nineteenth century, and all carried out in cast iron.

McFarlane's *Castings Catalogue* of 1874 gives a bewildering number of designs for these day-to-day necessities, upon which it was felt not wasteful to lavish every kind of decoration from the simplest to the most elaborate variations of 'antique' styles. Among the many other objects in this catalogue there are 475 designs for gutters and 486 for ventilation panels. Sometimes drainage pipes cross the pavement, and these gave another opportunity for many a fancy design (Plate 88).

Old pavement lights are distinguishable by always being framed in cast iron, whereas modern versions are set into concrete. The early iron frames are plain or ornamented and either filled entirely with little squares, oblongs or honeycombs of thick glass. These are also interspersed with iron ventilation holes, often in a checker-board pattern. If they hinge at one side, many of these 'lights' also serve as entries to basements.

All sizes and shapes of solid or framed iron inspection covers abound—for fire hydrants, telephone wires, gas and water mains—while the larger ones in the road give access to sewers, pipes and cables. The size of these has recently been of some concern to the authorities: in 1970 the government was worried that the old sewer covers were not strong enough to support the increasing amount of heavy traffic, particularly the Continental juggernauts thundering along our roads, so they set up a committee to discuss the matter; but even after several years it still could not decide how much stronger new covers needed to be. The committee did, how-

Plate 88 A typical finely decorated gutter, and a drainpipe covering which crosses a pavement in Falmouth, Cornwall (*Robert Enever*)

ever, recommend a new standard cover, larger than existing ones, though that had nothing to do with strength. As so many deaths are caused by poisonous gases underground, it was realised that the old smaller holes made rescue more difficult. Governments have a fondness for sitting on such holes: another committee considering those on building sites was still sitting in 1972 after 8 years, and another on the pavement variety sat for no less than 20—with little to show for it.

The most interesting category of underfoot street furniture is the coal-hole cover (Plate 89). These were (and still are, although to a lesser extent) to be found in the pavements outside houses that have cellars under the road. When one sees an old pavement with such covers still in place in front of modern buildings, one knows that here once stood a row of nineteenth-century private houses. Now that coal is no longer tipped into basements, these covers have

Plate 89 The snowflake-like range of iron coal-hole covers dating from 1863 (*Author*)

become obsolete, and when streets are demolished or altered the covers are often just thrown away, unless a preservation-minded collector or antique dealer is quick enough to rescue them.

With a few exceptions, these covers are no more than a foot in diameter. As well as being the only holes whose covers cannot slip down into them, they are also said to have been made this small to prevent a burglar making an easy entry; although perhaps an Oliver Twist might have managed it. They are all made of cast

iron and most date from 1863, although there is one outside an 1820 house in Norland Square in London's Shepherd's Bush that might be as old as the building. As with inspection covers, they were usually given a raised pattern to prevent pedestrians slipping on the shiny surface. These iron circles gave the Victorians—never really in need of one—a heavensent excuse to use their decorative imaginations. And decorative they certainly are.

The designs vary from the very ornate—stars, snow crystals and

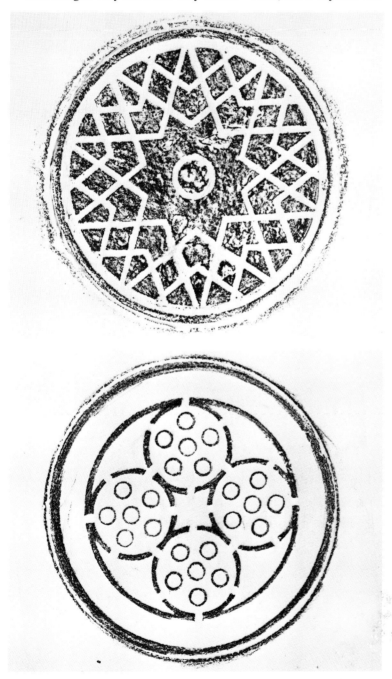

the inevitable Gothic design, often in the form of a simple or elaborate trefoil or quatrefoil—to more severe horizontal or criss-crossed lines, brick formations, mazes and many variations on the cricle (there is a lovely checkerboard one in Portland Place in London). Then there are those that also bear the maker's name or the name and style (such as 'Patent Self Locking'), or this lettering is the sole decoration. An interesting example of advertis-

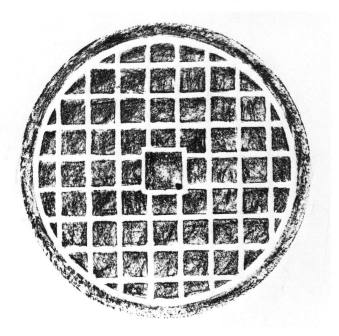

ing is to be found in the Southwark district of London which, contains some covers made by the iron and steel merchants J. W. Cunningham & Co, which carry the representation of a dog eating out of a pot. In London some of the most interesting are to be found in the York stone paving outside houses in Kensington, Pimlico, Paddington and Bloomsbury. Some rather grand ones were also made for special patrons, such as the simple but elegant covers in King Street and Duke Street in London, outside the premises of the famous medallists and numismatists Spink & Son, this name being carried out in brass letters. There is also a square one (not an unusual shape for a coal-cover) made entirely of this material with the words 'Harris, Hair Cutter' on it in St James's Square.

This is not to say that coal-covers are by any means confined to London. They turn up in cities, towns or villages—wherever, in fact, there are coal cellars in the basements outside private houses— and in the same variety of patterns as the London examples.

Of all pieces of street furniture, these covers seem to have attracted the most ardent devotees. As early as 1863, the year of their inception, Shephard Taylor, a 24-year-old medical student at King's College Hospital in London, became fascinated by them and decided to make a serious survey. The result was a small book containing 150 different designs—the decorative ones only, as Mr Taylor ignored the lettered ones or those which have 'lights' or ventilation holes let into them. Mr Taylor (later Dr) did not employ the comparatively easy method of taking a rubbing, but made very accurate line drawings. So familiar did he become with his subject that he claimed he could recognise the slightest variation on sight. He even coined a name for his obsession—opercula—which he took from the Latin *operculum*, meaning a cover, covering or lid. For good measure it is also a word used by zoologists to denote the entrance to a mollusc's shell or the protection over a fish's gills.

Despite his enthusiasm, official interest lapsed until as late as 1962, when an exhibition of rubbings and covers was held at Gallery One in North Audley Street in London. It was organised by the painter, poet and gallery owner Victor Musgrave, and opened by Mr (now Sir) John Betjeman. Devotee of all things Victorian, he naturally waxed fervently about the covers and lamented their passing. In the following year John Beales staged an exhibition of rubbings by Roger Greenwood at the Edinburgh Festival. In 1971 the London Museum (then in Kensington Palace, now at the Barbican) put on an exhibition of rubbings by schoolchildren (many schools still encourage this pastime) as well as photographs; the Museum itself possesses a number of good examples.

Many antique shops now sell either rubbings or the covers themselves. As well as being bought by British enthusiasts, they are sought after by Americans, who have them polished to hang on their walls or use them to make 'quaint' stepping stones in their gardens.

Mounting Blocks

Together with horse troughs and tethering posts, mounting blocks speak of a lost horse-oriented age. These stone or wooden stepped structures were made for those not agile enough to mount a horse unaided, by women in long skirts, by those ascending the high steps of a carriage or stagecoach and by men who had to hump heavy loads on to carts (Plate 90).

Although obsolete, there are still quite a number of them around. Some early ones were made out of other objects: for example, the very old and rare Mithraic altar that now stands in the church at Stone in Kent was at one time converted into a mounting block, and still carries the tethering ring often found on the 'real thing'. Another interesting conversion is a red sandstone mounting block that for many years was considered to have been originally a piece of Roman carving. It now stands outside the gate of Tullie House Museum in Abbey Street in Carlisle, which must go a long way to ensure its preservation. W. Hutchinson, in his 1794 *History of Cumberland* referred to it as 'a man playing upon bagpipes', and it was then part of a doorpost at Stanwix in the same county. By 1802 it had been moved and was seen by William Hutton, who described it in his *History of the Roman Wall* as 'a stone in the street, converted into a horse-block, three steps high, with the figure of a man, in a recess, eighteen inches in height, in a Roman dress, and in great preservation. I wonder', he continued, 'the boys had not pelted him out of the world.' If one compares the engraved illustrations in his book, where the carving is quite

Plate 90 Impossible to date, but, judging by its condition, probably at least eighteenth-century, this mounting block was once in great use outside the Lion and Lamb inn at Horsley, Northumberland (*Barbara Denness*)

distinct, with its present blurred state, one is led to suppose that many generations of boys (and others) have done exactly what Mr Hutton feared. He asked local elderly people what they knew of the stone's history but received the usual answer to such questions: it had 'stood there before my time'. Mr Hutton believed the figure to represent a 'Roman Chief' but its clothes and the presence of bagpipes suggest a seventeenth- or eighteenth-century peasant. The stone was subsequently lost, found again in 1878 and put in its present position in 1884.

Perhaps the most famous mounting block is that outside the Athenaeum in London, which was for the sole use of the 1st Duke of Wellington. Other less exalted ones were usually placed outside big houses, inns, churches, mills or warehouses. Being so utilitarian and not exactly works of art, most are impossible to date, and could have been made from 100 to several hundred years ago. Among the few dated examples is a two-step one on the roadside at Aston-le-Wall in Northamptonshire, which carries the following inscription: 'Thomas Height, of Warden, set this up, July the 30, 1659.' Another, standing in the old stables at the Wellington Inn at Riding Mill in Northumberland, could have been made in 1660 when the building, originally a miller's house, was put up. This block has five steps with a long platform, and such platforms are very usual outside mills, warehouses and on roads used by heavy transport, where they facilitated the loading of sacks or other large containers on to carts or waggons. The block outside the old Gibraltar Mill at Great Bardfield in Essex is of this type, being made out of old millstones that are said to be 200 years old.

Naturally enough few wooden mounting blocks survive but there is still a two-stepped one complete with platform and steadying post outside a church at Epping Upland in Essex, which was apparently popular with women who rode sidesaddle; old ladies today can remember using them before the days of jodhpurs—and the Queen still rides sidesaddle at the Trooping of the Colour ceremony on Horseguards Parade. There is a very worn set of stone steps outside the church at Bolam in Northumberland, and another, made out of a single block of stone as opposed to the usual series of slabs, inside the churchyard. Most mounting blocks have the steps to one side only but one with four steps at each end stands near the church at Lowther in Cumbria. A much worn mounting block, which now rests against the church wall at Boston in Lincolnshire, was originally a milestone, as it registers the distance to London—100 miles.

Footscrapers and Railings

Nowadays it is hard even for country people to realise just how filthy our roads and streets used to be, and for those in towns and cities it is even more difficult; but the fact is brought home if one notices how many footscrapers are still to be found at the entrances of houses. Although many are damaged and no one has considered them worth while repairing, there are still some excellent examples, varying from the primitive to the elegantly elaborate—the latter usually fine examples of the ironsmith's art and craft. As with street signs, most villages seem to have a prevailing pattern—with the odd individual one—whereas the variety in towns seems endless. In Harley Street, in London, which consists of mainly late eighteenth-century houses, I have counted at least thirty different styles.

The simplest form of scraper is merely an iron bar let into a cavity in the wall of a house (Plate 91); the most elaborate, with fine supports, is incorporated into the iron railings on the steps leading up to the front door (Plate 92) and in between comes a

Plate 91 A simple iron-plate footscraper let into the wall of a house at Fleet in Dumfries and Galloway, Scotland (*Barbara Denness*)

Plate 92 At the other end of the scale, this scraper is supported by fine, beautifully executed, twirls on a Regency house in London's Harley Street (*Author*)

plethora of shapes, styles and sizes (Plates 93–95). The cavity-in-the-wall variety is often made more elaborate by being given a cast-iron arch, or the arch itself is carved into an interesting shape. Sometimes the cavity contains a little free-standing iron scraper, and the cavity is not always in the wall of the house but at the base of the front steps. Many free-standing examples are to be found on steps or on pavements, and it is these that have suffered most through damage and neglect. As to style, they come Classic (appropriately severe outside the Athenaeum in London), Gothic, or in any mixture of the two.

More durable and likely to last are those let into railings. At the beginning of World War II there was a wholesale removal of many fine house, church and park railings and gates to provide iron for the 'war effort'. We thus lost some of our finest ironwork and one

Plate 93 A pretty type of footscraper, let into railings in Lowther Street, Whitehaven, Cumbria (*Barbara Denness*)

Plate 94 A sturdy type of footscraper: free-standing at the bottom of some steps. Falmouth, Cornwall (*Robert Enever*)

Plate 95 An amusing
footscraper at the door of the
Murray Arms Hotel in Fleet,
Dumfries and Galloway,
Scotland (*Barbara Denness*)

cannot help wondering just how much such 'vandalism' really
did contribute to victory. But railings whose removal would have
been dangerous, such as those on steps and around basement areas,
had to be spared. As so many footscrapers were fitted to these railings
they are still with us.

Although the design of railings is a large subject I have included
a few photographs (Plates 96–100). Eighteenth-century and
Regency ones are, naturally enough, to be found around the areas
or on steps of houses of the same period, but others have been
spared around such parks as Hyde Park and around the Nash
Terraces in Regent's Park. The simplest of this period use Classic
motifs: urns, and spears, both flat and in the round. With the
advent of the Victorian age every period was ransacked for ideas.
The Arts and Crafts Movement of the 1870s and 1880s and the
Art Nouveau craze of the 1890s to the 1910s produced a number
of original designs, although no English ones can rival the Paris
Metro entrances of this period for imagination and fancifulness.

Plate 96 Regency elegance and restraint: spears and an urn (*Author*)

Plate 97 Victorian Gothic with fleurs-de-lys spikes and barley-sugar posts (*Geoffrey N. Wright*)

Plate 98 More Victorian Gothic—fierce, warding-off spikes (*Author*)

Plate 99 Imaginative Arts and Crafts Movement railings (*Author*)

Plate 100 Heavy, stolid and unimaginative Edwardian railings—made to last (*Author*)

Bibliography

As yet there is no book entirely devoted to street furniture. These books and periodicals, therefore, deal—sometimes only in part—with one or more than one category.

Accum, Frederick. *A Practical Treatise on Gas-Light* (1815)

Anon, *Arguments against light* (Cologne, 1816)

Bebbington, Gillian. *London Street Names* (Batsford, 1972)

Beckmann, Joseph. *A History of Inventions, Discoveries and Origins*, Vol III, translated by William Johnson (1846)

Betjeman, John. *Victorian and Edwardian London from Old Photographs* (Batsford, 1969). There are other cities, towns and counties in this series

Bland, John. *Odd and Unusual England* (John Bland, 1974)

Briggs, Asa. *Victorian Cities* (Odhams, 1965; Penguin, 1968)

Coe, Brian and Millward, Michael. *Victorian Landscape* (1974)

Doolittle, William H. *Inventions of the Century* (Scott and Chambers, 1903)

Farrugia, Jean Young. *The Letter Box* (Centaur, 1969)

Ford, A. S. *Springs, Wells, Streams and Spas of London* (Fisher-Unwin, 1910)

Grigson, Geoffrey. *The Shell Country Alphabet* (Michael Joseph, 1966)

Harrison, Michael. *London Beneath the Pavement* (1961)

Hibbert, Christopher. *London, the Biography of a City* (Longmans, 1969)

Hobhouse, Hermione. *A History of Regent Street* (Macdonald and Jane's, 1975)

Johnson, Derek, E. *Essex Curiosities* (Spurbooks, 1973)

Lampton, Lucinda. *Vanishing Victoriana* (Elsevier/Phaidon, 1976)

Lea, Raymond. *Country Curiosities* (Spurbooks, 1973)

Lister, Raymond. *Opercula—London Coal Plates*, edited by 'Julia Aespulapuius' (The Golden Head Press, Cambridge, 1965)

——. *Decorative Cast Iron Work in Great Britain* (Bell, 1960)

Luckiesh, M. *Artificial Light—Influence upon Civilisation* (New York, 1920)

Matthews, William. *A Compendium of Gas-Lighting* (1827)

——. *Hydraulia* (1835)

——. *A Sketch of the Principal Means which have been Employed to Ameliorate the Intellectual and Moral Condition of the Working Classes in Birmingham*, pamphlet (1830)

Mitchell, R. J. and Leys, M. D. R. *A History of London Life* (1958)

O'Dea, William T. *The Social History of Lighting* (Science Museum Publication (1958 ed)

Pugin, Augustus Welby. *Contrasts* (1846)

Reader, W. J. *Victorian England* (1963)

Ridley, Anthony. *Living in Cities* (Heinemann, 1971)

Robins. F. W. *The Story of the Lamp (and the Candle)* 1937)

——. *The Story of Water Supply* (1946)

Robinson, Howard. *British Post Office* (1953)

Routh, Johnathan. *The Good Loo Guide* (Wolfe, 1965)

Russell, George E. (Ed). *Sir Wilfred Lawson* (1909)

——. *Signs of the Times* (Elm Tree Books, 1974)

Sunderland, W. *Old London Spas, Baths and Wells* (Bale, 1915)

Tims, John. *Stories of Inventions and Discoveries in Science and the Useful Arts*, I (1860)

——. *Treasures of Britain* (AA Drive Publications, 1972)

Whitehead, David. *London Then, London Now* (1949)

Whittaker, W. *The Water Supply of Kent* (HMSO, 1908); *Surrey* (HMSO, 1912); *Essex* (HMSO, 1916); *Buckinghamshire and Hertfordshire* (HMSO, 1921)

Wright, Lawrence. *Clean and Decent* (Routledge & Kegan Paul, 1960)

PERIODICALS

Builder, The (1846–91)

Building News (1893)

Country Life

Field, The

Illustrated London News, The

Monthly Magazine, The (1807)

SELECT LIST OF IRON-FOUNDERS' ETC, CATALOGUES

Gardiner, Sons & Co, Ltd, Bristol

Ironmonger Diary and Text Book, The, London

Macfarlane's Castings, Glasgow

Parket, Winder & A. Church Ltd, Birmingham

Smith and Founders' Directory (1823)

Acknowledgements

I am particularly indebted to Mrs Barbara Denness, not only for supplying me with many of the photographs which appear in this book (and those which only lack of space prevents me from using) but also for a great deal of information, field-work, research and for giving me a number of useful 'leads'. Not least for her interest, enthusiasm and encouragement. I must also thank my twin brother Roger, of the Ancient Monuments Department of the Ministry of the Environment, for reading the typescript, making pertinent comments and checking many points for me.

My thanks are also due to the many archivists, county record officers, librarians, secretaries, town clerks etc, as well as various bodies connected with the preservation and historical aspects of the subject, who are too many to list.

The author and publishers wish particularly to thank the following for their help in writing this book; Assistant County Archivist, Somerset Record Office; Assistant County Librarian, North Yorkshire County Library; Assistant Keeper of Antiquities, Newarke Houses Museum, Leicester; Borough Librarian, London Borough of Richmond upon Thames; Borough Librarian and Curator, London Borough of Southwark; City Architect and Planning Officer, City of Cambridge; City Archivist, City Clerk's Department, Bristol; County Archivist, County Record Office, Northumberland; Curator, City Museum and Art Gallery, Gloucester; District Planning Officer, Planning Department, Grantham; Richard Emerson, Royal Commission on the Ancient and Historical Monuments of Scotland; C. R. Levington, former Town Clerk, Borough of Blandford Forum, Dorset; Public Lighting Officer, Commercial Sales Department, North Thames Gas; and Senior Assistant Archivist. County Record Office, Durham.

Index

Page numbers in italics indicate illustrations

Albion Ironworks, Westminster, 134
Ancient Monuments, Department of the Environment, 12, 36
Annals of Windsor, 21
Argument Against Light, 73

Betjeman, Sir John, 11, 143
bollards, Carlisle, Cumbria, 128; Drewsteignton, Devon, 128; Hexham, Northumberland, 127; London, 124, 125, *124, 125;* Market Harborough, Leicestershire, 128; Queen's Square, London, 127; Swanage, Dorset, 128; Whitehaven, Cumbria, 125, *126;* reproduction, 128-9; wooden: Canterbury, 125, Penrith, Cumbria, 125, Warwick, 125, Wells, 125
Builder, The, 67

cabbies' shelters, Ipswich, 133; London: Brompton Road, 133, Leicester Square, 133, The Temple, 133; Suffolk, 133
Camden Historical Society, The, 70
Carron, Co, Falkirk, Scotland, 124
Cast Iron & Pump Founders & Engineers, 26
Castle Museum, York, 12
Chadwick, Edwin, 67
Chalybeate water, 19
Civic Trust, The, 12
clocks, Abinger Hammer, Surrey, 103; Amersham, Bucks, 103; Bishop Auckland, Co Durham, 105; Brampton, Cumbria, 103; Carfax, Oxford, 104; Chester, 105, *104;* Coalbrookdale, Salop, 104; Cookham, Bucks, 102;

Exeter, Devon, 104; Felstead, Essex, 103; Great Dunmow, Essex, 104; Great Holland, Essex, 104; London: Old Kent Road, 103; Northill, Beds, 102; St Leonard-at-the-Hythe, Essex, 102; Sutton, Courtney, Oxfordshire, 102; Wallingford, Oxfordshire, 103; Whitgift, Humberside, 103
clocks, bracket, Canterbury, 109; Colchester, Essex, 108; Falmouth, Cornwall, 108; Guildford, Surrey, 108; London: Southampton Street, 109, Kilburn High Road, 109; Longbridge Deverill, Wilts, 108; York, 109-10, *109*
clock towers, Brighton, Sussex, 105, *106;* Creetown, Scotland, 108; Crickdale, Wilts, 106; Epsom, Surrey, 107; Grimstone, Norfolk, 106; London: Big Ben, 105; Machynlleth, Powys, 105; Rhayader, Powys, 107; St Andrews, Scotland, 106; Swanage, Dorset, 105; Tynemouth, Tyne and Wear, *107,* Wendover, Bucks, 107
coal-hole covers, 138-43, *139, 140, 141, 142*
Cochrane & Co, 96
conduit heads, Bristol, 31; 'Carfax', Oxford, 35-6; Chelmsford, 36-7, *37;* Durham, Co Durham, 31-5, *32, 33;* Edinburgh, Scotland, 37; Grantham, Lincs, 37-8; 'Hobsons', Cambridge, 35; Leicester, 30; 'Scrivens', Gloucester, 36
Contrasts, 27
Council for the Protection of Rural England, 11, 12

Dean & Co, 78
Davy, Sir Humphrey, 89
Dockwar, William, 94
drinking fountains, Allendale, Northumberland, 51; Alston, Cumbria, 59; Aspatria, Cumbria, *45,* 46; Bamburgh, Northumberland, 53, *54;* Bath, 46; Billingham, Northumberland, 51; Cambo, Northumberland, *61;* Corsham, Wilts, 50; Creetown, Scotland, 61; Cullercoats, Tyne and Wear, 50-1, *51;* Darlington, Co Durham, *60,* 60-1; Dawley, Salop, 50; Dudley, Leicestershire, 43-4; Gatehouse-of-Fleet, Scotland, *58;* Grasmere, Lake District, *49;* Hexham, Northumberland, 52, 55, 57; Jedburgh, Scotland, 51; Lee, Bucks, 51; London: Adelaide Street, 42, Drury Lane Theatre, *48,* Fitzjohn's Avenue, 18, Holborn Viaduct, 39-41, *39,* Royal Exchange, 41, 42, Shaftesbury Avenue, 52, Victoria Gardens, 49, West End Land, 53; Middleton-in-Teesdale, 56; Nenthead, Cumbria, *55,* 56; Newcastle: 47, Jesmond Road, 51; Richmond, Greater London, 59; Riding Hall, Northumberland, 54; Ripley, N Yorks, 61; Shildon, Co Durham, *56,* 57; Staindrop, Co Durham, 53; Warwick, 57; Wharton, Northumberland, 57; Whitehaven, Cumbria, 53, 57; White Waltham, Berks, 52; Wigton, Cumbria, 53; York, 12
duty posts, 119

Electric lighting, early history, 87-8; Hungerford Bridge, London, 87; Liverpool, 87; America, 88; bracket lamps: 78-9, Bath, 91, 'blue lamps', 91, 'Burning Bush', Eton, Berks, 91, London: 'Cheshire Cheese', Fleet Street, 91, Drury Lane Theatre, 91, Hyde Park, 91, 'Red Lion', Kilburn High Road, 89, Royal Arcade, Pall Mall, 91, over arch, Carlisle, Cumbria, 90, shop window, *90*, Tunbridge Wells, Kent, 91
Express, The, 12

Farrugia, Mrs Jean Young, 96
footscrapers, Falmouth, Cornwall, *148;* Fleet, Scotland, 146, *149;* Harley Street, London, 146, *147;* Whitehaven, Cumbria, *148*

Gas, Light & Coke Co, 77
gas lighting, Barnes Pool Bridge, Eton, Berks, 81; Birmingham, 79; Brighton, 80; Canterbury, 80; Egham, Surrey, 11; 'English' Bridge, Shrewsbury, 81; Falmouth, Cornwall, 82; Liverpool, 79; London: Admiralty Arch, 84, *85,* Carlton House Terrace, 79, Charing Cross Road, *84,* Covent Garden, 11, 73, Lambeth Bridge, 81, Long Acre, 85, Paddington, 79, Pall Mall, 17, St James' Park, 79, Serpentine Bridge, 81, The Temple, 82, Trafalgar Square, 84, *85,* Westminster, 79, Westminster Bridge, 81; Oxford: 79, New College Lane, 78; Southend, 79; Taunton Bridge, Devon, 81; York: Lendal Bridge, 80, Ouse Bridge, 81
Gay, John, 76
George, Smith & Co, Sun Foundry, Glasgow, 70
Glenfield & Kennedy, Kilmarnock, Scotland, 28, 55
gratings, 137-8

hansom cabs, 131-2
Hemming, Edward, 74
History of Cornwall, 17
House and shop numbers, 131

Ironmonger, Diary & Text Book, The, 137

Jennings, George, 66-7, 71, 72

King's Reach, London, *86, 87*
lamplighters, 81-3
Lawson, Sir Wilfrid, 46
London Directory, The, 26

Macfarlane's Casting Catalogue, 137
Macfarlane, Glasgow, 10, 59
McDowell Steven & Co, Architectural Iron Founders, Glasgow, 71
Metropolitan Drinking Fountain and Cattle Trough Association, 18, 40, 42
milestones, Alconby Hill, Cambs, 114; Atherstone, Warks, 118; Brampton, Cambs, 116; Bredon, Herefordshire, 116; Cambridge to Barkway, 113; Chalfont St Peters', Bucks, 111; Chatteris, Cambs, 118; East Hoathly, Sussex, 115; East Wycombe, Bucks, 114; Esher, Surrey, 114; Fairmile, Devon, 117; 'Gout Track', 117; Holt, Norfolk, 114; London: Highgate Hill, 112 Knightsbridge, 117, 'The Obelisk', St Georges' Road, 116; 'Tyburn' stone, 116; Newbold-on-Stour, Warks, 117, *118;* New Forest, Hants, 115; North Cave, Humberside, 118; Otterton, Devon, 114; Oxford Road, 113; 'Pudding' stones, 111; Richmond, Greater London, 116; Roman, 112; Rye, Kent, 113; Shaftesbury, Dorset, 114; Sheffield Park, Sussex, 114; Telford stones, 117; Thirsk, N Yorks, 118; West Wycombe, Bucks, 114
mounting blocks, Aston-le-Wall, Northants, 145; Bolam, Northumberland, 145; Boston, Lincs, 145; Epping Upland, Essex, 145; Great Bradfield, Essex, 145; Horsley, Northants, 144; London: Athenaeum, 145; Lowther, Cumbria, 145; Riding Mill, Northumberland, 145; 'Roman', 144-5; Stone, Kent, 144

Murdock, William, 76

Nash, Beau, 28
National Monument Library, 12
National Motor Museum, Beaulieu, 129
New River Company, 41

'Pants', explanations of, 53-4
Pevensy, Nicholas, 53
pillar boxes, 'Anonymous', Falmouth, Cornwall, *97;* early history, 93; 'Early Mainland', Barnes Cross, Dorset, 93; 'Doric Column', *96;* first London pillar box, 94; Ilkley, N Yorks, *96,* 97; 'National Standard', 97; 'Penfold', York, 12; 'The Pillar Box Treasure Hunt', 96; 'Window Men', 95; Wooden boxes, 95
plague stones, Bury St Edmunds, 123, *123;* Leeds, 123; Penrith, Cumbria, 123
porters' rests, 133
public lavatories, Bath, 71; Birmingham, 69; Bristol, Avon, *68,* 69; Cambridge, 71; Crystal Palace; at Hyde Park, 67, at Sydenham, 67; Dumfries, Scotland, 69; Great Ayton, N Yorks, 69; Housesteads, Hadrian's Wall, Northumberland, 66; London: Cheyne Walk, Chelsea, 70, Holborn, 71, Holborn Viaduct, 71, Kensington Gardens, 72, Leicester Square, 72, Park Lane, 70, Star Yard, Chancery Lane, 70, Turnham Green, 72, West End Lane, 72; Reading, 69; Stafford, 72; Walkerburn, Scotland, 69, 70; at Wellington's funeral, 67
Pugin, Augustus, 27
pumps, Alcomb, Northumberland, 28; Allendale, Northumberland, 28; Blandford Forum, Dorset, 25; Cambridge: Rose Street, 24; Carsphairn, Scotland, *23;* Castle Combe, Wilts, 28; Clacton-on-Sea, Essex, 29; Corfe, Dorset, 25; Dorchester, Dorset, 28; Durham, Co Durham, *27;* Faringdon, Oxfordshire, 27; Farrington, Glos, 25; Hampton Lucy,

Warks, 25; Hemel Hempstead, Herts, 28; Latimer, Bucks/ Herts, 28; London: Bedford Row, 24, Cornhill, *24,* Queen's Square, 24, The Museum of, 22; Newborough, Northumberland, *29;* Poyle, Berks, 29; Salisbury Museum, 22; South Wold, Suffolk, 26; Tichnell, Derbyshire, 28; Watton-at-Stone, Herts, 28; Wells, Somerset, 28

railings, Arts and Crafts, *151;* Edwardian, *151;* Regency, *150;* Victorian Gothic, *150, 151*
Rowlandson, William, 77, *77*
Royal Commission on the Ancient and Historical Monuments of Scotland, 12, 70

Saracen, Foundry, Glasgow, 70
Science Museum, 12
seats, Bullgill, Cumbria, 135; Burley, Hants, 134; Hexham, Northumberland, *135;* London: Victoria Embankment, 134, *135,* Victoria Park, Hackney, 134; Ryde, Isle of Wight, 133; Seahouses, Northumberland, *136*
signposts, Basset's Pole, Staffs, 119; Bath, 122; Breadsall, Derbyshire, 121; Bristol: 'Three Lamps', 120; Broadway Hill, Worcs, 119; Brownhill, Staffs, 120; Little Brampton, Salop, *120;* London: Hackney, 122, 123; Newborough, Northants, 121,

122; Norton Lindsey, Warks, *121;* Staindrop, Co Durham, 122; Teddington Hands, Glos, 119
Smith and Founders Directory, The, 10, 83
snuffers, Alfred Street, Bath, *75,* 76; Berkeley Square, London, *75,* 76
stamp vending machines, 98; Falmouth, Cornwall, *98*
street names, rampton, Cumbris, *130;* London, Abbey Road, 131, North London, 130
sundials, mass dials, 99; Appleby, Cumbria, 102; Carlisle, Cumbria, 100; Great Staughton, Cambs, 102; Isleworth, Greater London, 100; Kellaways, Wilts, 102; Long Wittenham, Oxfordshire 99; North Stoke, Oxfordshire, 99; Petts Wood, Greater London, 102; St Wenn, Cornwall, 100; Weobely, Hereford & Worcester, *99*

Tailors and Chandlers Company, 74-5, 78
Taxi Drivers Association, 131
Telford, Thomas, 115
Temperance Movement, The, 44-7
Treaty of Amiens, 76
Trollope, Anthony, 93
troughs, Harwich Road, Essex, 63; London: Carlton Hill, 64, *65,* Hopton Street, Southwark, 64, Little Venice, Maida Vale, 63; Penzance, Cornwall, 64-5, *65;* Richmond, Greater London, 64

Turnpike Acts, 115

Vanburgh, Sir John, 18
Victoria Embankment, London 85-6, *86,* 87
Victorian Society, The, 12

wall-boxes, 97-8; Hexham, Northumberland, *98;* Newport, Isle of Wight, 98
warning signs, 'Dead Slow' Rushbrooks, Suffolk, *129;* London: Abbey Road, 129; Padstow, Cornwall, 129; St Just, Cornwall, 129
wells, Aldworth, Berks, 20; Barmouth, Wales, 22; Carrawburgh, Northumberland, 16; Cradle Well, Jesmond, Tyne and Wear, *20,* 21; Derry Hall, Wilts, 20; Digby, Lincs, 18; Doncaster, N Yorks, 18; Fawley Green, Bucks, 20; Holywell, Cambs, 17; Holywell, Clywd, 19; Holy Well, Malvern, 19; Rebecca's Well, Wargrave, Berks, 20; Royston, Herts, 20; St Anne's, Caversham, Reading, 19; St Carantocus, Cornwall, 17; St Dominic, Cornwall, 17; St Edith's, Kemsing, Kent, 19; St Keynes, Cornwall, 18; St Winifred's, Woolston, Salop, 18; Upway, Dorset, 18; Veryan, Cornwall, *17;* Windsor, Berks, 21
well dressings, 19
Winsor, Albert, 77-8
Wright, Nathaniel, 24

Thursford
George Cushing